21

Baking
Is
Fun

Volume 2

Contents

Recipes   Page

Recipe Index

4

5

After the success of our "Baking is Fun" Volume 1, we feel encouraged to now publish Volume 2. We have searched in Austria, Germany and Switzerland to find more of the traditional authentic recipes which have been handed down from one generation to the other for centuries. The result is a unique collection of truly European baking specialties. All of them have been tested and adapted to locally available ingredients. Recipes are given in both European metric and Canadian imperial measures.

In many recipes we suggest the use of more **oetker** products as did the original recipes, because in Europe **oetker** has been supplying housewives with quality baking ingredients for generations. Therefore, to give you the optimum flavour of real European baking, we suggest you follow the original tradition and use **oetker** ingredients.

Happy baking in the true European tradition!

Yours sincerely,
oetker RECIPE SERVICE

Marzipan Torte

Sponge Batter:

5	egg yolks	5
150 g	sugar	¾ cup
1 pkg	**oetker** vanilla sugar	1 pkg.
5	egg whites	5
110 g	all-purpose flour	¾ cup
1 g	**oetker** baking powder	¼ tsp.
10 g	cocoa	1 tbsp.
5 mL	cinnamon	1 tsp.
pinch	ground cloves	pinch
10 mL	instant coffee powder	2 tsp.
30 g	ground walnuts	¼ cup

Filling:

1 btl	**oetker** rum flavouring concentrate	1 btl.
15 mL	lemon juice	1 tbsp.
250 g	almond paste or marzipan	8 oz.
100 g	icing sugar	¾ cup
30 mL	apricot jam or marmalade	2 tbsp.

Chocolate Cream:

150 g	sweet (unsalted) butter	¾ cup
100 g	sifted icing sugar	¾ cup
1 pkg	**oetker** vanilla sugar	1 pkg.
1	egg yolk	1
4 sq	semi-sweet chocolate, melted	4 sq.
30 g	cocoa	¼ cup

Decoration:

4 sq	semi-sweet chocolate, grated	4 sq.
	whole candied cherries	

Sponge Batter:

PREHEAT oven to 180°C (350°F). Grease a 24 cm (9½") spring form pan and line with waxed paper.
COMBINE egg yolks, sugar and vanilla sugar in mixer bowl. Beat at high speed of electric mixer until thick and creamy.
BEAT egg whites to stiff peaks.
SIFT flour, baking powder, cocoa, cinnamon, ground cloves and instant coffee powder together. Stir in walnuts. Fold into egg yolk mixture gently but thoroughly.
FOLD in egg whites gently.
SPREAD batter evenly in prepared pan.
BAKE on middle oven rack at 180°C (350°F) for 30-35 minutes or until toothpick inserted in centre comes out clean.
REMOVE from pan immediately. Remove waxed paper and let cake cool completely.
SLICE cake horizontally to make 2 layers.

Filling:

MIX rum flavouring concentrate and lemon juice.
KNEAD almond paste and icing sugar until smooth. Divide into 2 equal portions. Roll out each portion to size of cake layers.
DRIZZLE both cake layers with rum and lemon mixture.
COVER bottom cake layer with almond paste layer, setting second almond paste layer aside.
SPREAD evenly with apricot jam and cover with second cake layer.

Chocolate Cream:

CREAM butter. Gradually add icing sugar, vanilla sugar, egg yolk, melted chocolate and cocoa, beating until smoothly blended.
SPREAD part of the chocolate cream over top and sides of cake.
SPRINKLE sides with grated chocolate.
CUT second almond paste layer into wedges, starting from the middle, forming a star shape. DO NOT CUT COMPLETELY through, so that round shape is still intact.
COVER top layer of cake with almond paste layer. Roll up each wedge very carefully from the point to the outer edge of the cake.
SPRINKLE centre of cake with grated chocolate and decorate torte with remainder of chocolate cream and cherries.

Pineapple "Savoy" Cream Torte

Sponge Batter:

5	egg yolks	5
150 g	sugar	¾ cup
1 pkg	**oetker** vanilla sugar	1 pkg.
5	egg whites	5
110 g	all-purpose flour	¾ cup
1 g	**oetker** baking powder	¼ tsp.

Liquid Mixture:

150 mL	pineapple juice	⅔ cup
15 mL	lemon juice	1 tbsp.
45 mL	apricot brandy	3 tbsp.
45 mL	apricot jam or marmalade	3 tbsp.

Filling:

500 mL	whipping cream	2 cups
2 pkg	**oetker** Whip it	2 pkg.
1 pkg	**oetker** vanilla sugar	1 pkg.

Decoration:

6	pineapple slices maraschino cherries angelica	6

Sponge Batter:
PREHEAT oven to 180°C (350°F). Grease a 26 cm (10½") spring form pan and line with waxed paper.
COMBINE egg yolks, sugar and vanilla sugar in mixer bowl. Beat at high speed of electric mixer until thick and creamy.
BEAT egg whites to stiff peaks.
SIFT flour and baking powder together over egg yolk mixture. Fold in gently but thoroughly.
FOLD in egg whites gently.
SPREAD batter evenly in prepared pan.
BAKE on middle oven rack at 180°C (350°F) for 25-35 minutes or until toothpick inserted in centre comes out clean.
REMOVE from pan immediately. Remove waxed paper and let cake cool completely.
Filling:
MIX pineapple juice, lemon juice and apricot brandy. Drizzle over cake.
SPREAD evenly with apricot jam.
BEAT whipping cream to soft peaks. Gradually add Whip it and vanilla sugar. Continue beating until stiff.
DECORATE cake with whipped cream (using a decorating bag for an attractive finish), pineapple slices (halved), maraschino cherries and angelica.

Raspberry Cream Torte

Batter:

5	egg yolks	5
30 mL	hot water	2 tbsp.
150 g	sugar	¾ cup
1 pkg	**oetker** vanilla sugar	1 pkg.
3 drops	**oetker** almond flavouring concentrate	3 drops
5	egg whites	5
100 g	all-purpose flour	⅔ cup
8 g	**oetker** baking powder	2 tsp.
30 g	cocoa	⅓ cup
50 g	ground walnuts	½ cup

Filling:

200 g	frozen raspberries	1 cup
15 mL	lemon juice	1 tbsp.
1 pkg	**oetker** vanilla pudding mix	1 pkg.
125 g	sugar	⅔ cup
500 mL	milk	2 cups
250 g	sweet (unsalted) butter	1 cup

Batter:
PREHEAT oven to 180°C (350°F).
GREASE a 24 cm (9½") spring form pan. Line sides and base with waxed paper.
COMBINE egg yolks, hot water, sugar, vanilla sugar and almond flavouring together in a mixing bowl.
BEAT at high speed, with electric mixer until thick and creamy. In another bowl, beat egg whites to form stiff, but moist peaks.
SIFT flour, baking powder and cocoa together over egg yolk mixture.
FOLD in gently but thoroughly. Then fold in egg whites and nuts until combined.
TURN batter into prepared pan.
BAKE on lower oven rack for 35-40 minutes or until toothpick inserted in the centre comes out clean.
REMOVE from pan immediately. Remove waxed paper and let cake cool completely.
SLICE cake horizontally to make 3 even layers.

Continued on page 12.

Raspberry Cream Torte (cont.)

Decoration:

raspberries
chocolate sprinkles

Filling and Assembly:
PLACE raspberries in a bowl, sprinkle with lemon juice and let thaw at room temperature. Drain.
Combine **oetker** vanilla pudding mix, sugar and 125 mL (½ cup) milk in a small bowl. Stir until smoothly blended.
HEAT remaining 375 mL (1½ cups) milk to boiling in a saucepan.
STIR in pudding mixture. Bring to a boil, stirring constantly.
REMOVE from heat. Cool to room temperature, stirring occasionally.
CREAM butter. Beat in cooled pudding, one spoonful at a time. (Butter and pudding must be at the same temperature to prevent curdling.)
SET ASIDE a few raspberries for decoration. Fold remaining raspberries into pudding mixture.
SPREAD ¼ of filling on bottom cake layer. Cover with second layer.
SPREAD second ¼ of filling over second layer, cover with third layer.
Decoration:
SPREAD most of the remaining filling over the top and sides of the torte.
COVER the sides of the torte with chocolate sprinkles
DECORATE with remaining filling and raspberries.

Recipe No. 97

Strawberry Cream Torte

Batter:

150 g	sweet (unsalted) butter	¾	cup
150 g	sugar	¾	cup
1 pkg	**oetker** vanilla sugar	1	pkg.
3	egg yolks	3	
4 sq	semi-sweet chocolate, melted	4	sq.
150 g	all-purpose flour	1	cup
8 g	**oetker** baking powder	2	tsp.
3	egg whites	3	

Filling:

500 g	strawberries	1	lb.
125 mL	whipping cream	½	cup
1 pkg	**oetker** Whip it	1	pkg.
1 pkg	**oetker** vanilla sugar	1	pkg.
30 g	sifted icing sugar	⅓	cup

Decoration:

4 sq	semi-sweet chocolate, shaved	4	sq.
	strawberries		

Batter:
PREHEAT oven to 180°C (350°F). Grease and flour a 24 cm (9½") spring form pan.
CREAM butter and gradually add sugar, vanilla sugar egg yolks and melted chocolate.
SIFT flour and baking powder together and fold in gently but thoroughly.
BEAT egg whites to stiff peaks and fold into mixture gently.
TURN batter into prepared pan.
BAKE on lower oven rack at 180°C (350°F) for 30-40 minutes or until toothpick inserted in centre comes out clean.
REMOVE from pan immediately and let cake cool completely.
Filling:
SET a few strawberries aside for decoration. Puré remaining strawberries.
BEAT whipping cream to soft peaks. Gradually add Whip it, vanilla sugar and icing sugar. Continue beating until stiff.
FOLD strawberry purée into cream mixture.
SPREAD cream mixture evenly on cake.
COVER sides of cake with shaved chocolate.
DECORATE with strawberries.

Christmas Star

Batter:

4	egg yolks	4	
150 g	sugar	¾ cup	
1 pkg	**oetker** vanilla sugar	1 pkg.	
4	egg whites	4	
100 g	all-purpose flour	⅔ cup	
8 g	**oetker** baking powder	2 tsp.	
100 g	ground walnuts	1 cup	

Filling:

150 g	sweet (unsalted) butter	¾ cup	
100 g	icing sugar, sifted	¾ cup	
4 sq	semi-sweet chocolate, melted	4 sq.	
1 btl	**oetker** rum flavouring concentrate	1 btl.	
1	egg yolk	1	
50 mL	red lingonberry jam, raspberry jam or marmalade	¼ cup	

Glaze:

1 pkg	**oetker** Chocofix OR	1 pkg.	
6 sq	semi-sweet chocolate	6 sq.	
125 g	sweet (unsalted) butter	½ cup	

Decoration:

50 g	almond paste	¼ cup	
30 g	icing sugar	½ cup	
	silver candied beads		

Batter:
PREHEAT oven to180°C (350°F). Grease and flour a sta shaped pan.
COMBINE egg yolks, ⅔ of sugar and vanilla sugar in small mixer bowl. Beat at high speed of electric mixer unt thick and creamy.
BEAT egg whites and remaining sugar to stiff peaks.
MIX flour, baking powder and ground walnuts together. Fold into egg yolk mixture gently, but thoroughly.
FOLD egg whites into egg yolk mixture gently.
TURN into prepared pan.
BAKE on lower oven rack at 180°C (350°F) for 35-40 minutes or until toothpick inserted in centre comes out clean.
REMOVE from pan imediately and let cake cool completely.
SLICE cake horizontally to make 2 layers.
Filling:
CREAM butter. Gradually beat in icing sugar, melted chocolate, rum flavouring and egg yolk.
SPREAD bottom cake layer with jam.
SPREAD cream filling over jam.
PLACE top cake layer over filling.
Chocolate Glaze:
PREPARE Chocofix according to package directions OR COMBINE chocolate and butter in top of double boiler.
Place over boiling water. Stir constantly until smoothly melted.
SPREAD quickly over sides and top of cake.
KNEAD almond paste and icing sugar together until smooth.
ROLL out to 5 mm (¼″) thickness and cut out star shapes.
DECORATE cake with almond paste stars and silver candies.

Autumn Torte

Batter:

2	egg yolks	2	
30 mL	hot water	2 tbsp.	
100 g	sugar	½ cup	
1 pkg	**oetker** vanilla sugar	1 pkg.	
6 drops	**oetker** lemon flavouring concentrate	6 drops	
2	egg whites	2	
100 g	all-purpose flour	⅔ cup	
4 g	**oetker** baking powder	1 tsp.	

Batter:
PREHEAT oven to 180°C (350°F). Grease 24 cm (9½″) spring form pan. Line with waxed paper.
COMBINE egg yolks, hot water, ⅔ of sugar, vanilla sugar and lemon flavouring in mixer bowl. Beat at high speed o electric mixer until creamy.
BEAT egg whites and remaining sugar to stiff peaks.
SIFT flour and baking powder together over egg yolk mixture. Fold in gently but thoroughly.
FOLD egg whites gently into egg yolk mixture.
TURN batter into prepared pan.
BAKE on lower oven rack at 180°C (350°F) for 30-35 minutes or until toothpick inserted in centre comes out clean.
REMOVE from pan immediately. Remove waxed paper and let cake cool completely.
SLICE cake horizontally with thread to make 2 layers, the top layer only being 2 cm (¾″) thick.

Continued on page 16.

14

Autumn Torte (cont.)

Filling:

125 mL	red currant jam	½ cup	
1 pkg	**oetker** cheesecake filling mix with cardboard mould	1 pkg.	
500 mL	water	2 cups	
500 g	quark, ricotta or cream cheese	2 cups	
250 mL	whipping cream	1 cup	

Decoration:

2	kiwi fruits	2	
	green grapes		

Filling:
SPREAD half of jam on bottom cake layer.
WRAP cardboard mould tightly around layer.
COMBINE cheesecake filling mix and water and beat until foamy.
MIX quark or cheese until smooth. Gradually add to prepared filling mixture.
BEAT whipping cream to stiff peaks. Fold into cheese mixture.
SPREAD ⅔ of cheese filling evenly on bottom layer.
SPREAD remaining jam on second cake layer.
CUT layer in 12 equal size pieces and place over cheese filling.
DECORATE with remaining cheese filling.
REFRIGERATE and decorate sides of cake with sliced kiwis and grapes just before serving.

Recipe No. 100

Crunchy Caramel Torte

Batter:

5	egg yolks	5	
150 g	sugar	¾ cup	
1 pkg	**oetker** vanilla sugar	1 pkg.	
5	egg whites	5	
110 g	all-purpose flour	¾ cup	
1 g	**oetker** baking powder	¼ tsp.	

Filling:

1 pkg	**oetker** vanilla pudding mix	1 pkg.	
150 g	sugar	¾ cup	
375 mL	cold strong coffee	1½ cups	
125 mL	whipping cream	½ cup	
200 g	sweet (unsalted) butter	¾ cup	
1 tsp	cocoa	1 tsp.	
1 btl	**oetker** rum flavouring concentrate	1 btl.	

Caramel Mixture:

100 g	chopped almonds	⅔ cup	
30 g	sweet (unsalted) butter	3 tbsp.	
100 g	sugar	½ cup	

Decoration:

	maraschino cherries

Batter:
PREHEAT oven to 180°C (350°F). Grease a 24 cm (9½") spring form pan. Line with waxed paper.
COMBINE egg yolks, sugar and vanilla sugar in mixer bowl. Beat at high speed of electric mixer until thick and creamy.
BEAT egg whites to stiff peaks.
SIFT flour and baking powder together over egg yolk mixture. Fold in gently but thoroughly.
FOLD in egg whites gently.
SPREAD batter evenly in prepared pan.
BAKE on lower oven rack at 180°C (350°F) for 25-30 minutes.
REMOVE from pan immediately. Remove waxed paper and let cake cool completely.
SLICE cake horizontally with thread to make 2 layers.
Filling:
COMBINE pudding mix, sugar and 125 mL (½ cup) coffee in small bowl. Stir until blended.
RINSE saucepan with cold water.
HEAT remaining 250 mL (1 cup) coffee and whipping cream to boiling. Stir in pudding mixture, cocoa and rum flavouring. Bring to boil again, stirring constantly.
REMOVE from heat. Cool to room temperature, stirring occasionally.
CREAM butter. Beat in pudding, one spoonful at a time. (Butter and pudding must be at same temperature to prevent curdling.)
Caramel mixture:
Cook almonds in butter and sugar in a saucepan until caramelized. Let cool.
CRUSH into small pieces.
SPREAD ⅔ of filling on bottom cake layer.
SPRINKLE with part of the caramel mixture.
COVER with top cake layer.
SPREAD ⅔ of remaining filling over top and sides of cake.
COVER with remaining caramel mixture.
DECORATE top with rosettes of remaining filling and cherries.

Hazelnut Torte

Batter:

4	egg yolks	4	
30 mL	hot water	2	tbsp.
200 g	sugar	1	cup
1 pkg	**oetker** vanilla sugar	1	pkg.
4	egg whites	4	
80 g	all-purpose flour	½	cup
4 g	**oetker** baking powder	1	tsp.
100 g	ground hazelnuts	1	cup
50 g	fine dry bread crumbs	½	cup

Filling:
Chocolate cream:

200 g	sweet (unsalted) butter	1	cup
180 g	sifted icing sugar	1¼	cups
4 sq	semi-sweet chocolate, melted	4	sq.
1	egg	1	
1 btl	**oetker** rum flavouring concentrate	1	btl.

Frosting:
Hazelnut cream:

250 mL	whipping cream	1	cup
50 g	sifted icing sugar	⅓	cup
1 pkg	**oetker** vanilla sugar	1	pkg.
1 pkg	**oetker** Whip it	1	pkg.
100 g	ground hazelnuts	1	cup

Decoration:

	small chocolate leaves or thin chocolate wedges, optional

Batter:
PREHEAT oven to 180°C (350°F). Grease 24 cm (9½") spring form pan. Line with waxed paper.
COMBINE egg yolks, hot water, ⅔ of sugar and vanilla sugar in mixer bowl. Beat at high speed of electric mixer until thick and creamy.
BEAT egg whites and remaining sugar to stiff peaks.
FOLD into egg yolk mixture gently.
SIFT flour, baking powder, ground nuts and bread crumbs together over egg mixture. Fold in gently.
TURN batter into prepared pan.
BAKE on lower oven rack at 180°C (350°F) for 35-45 minutes or until toothpick inserted in centre comes out clean.
REMOVE from pan immediately. Remove waxed paper and let cake cool completely.
SLICE cake horizontally with thread to make 2 layers.
Chocolate cream:
CREAM butter and icing sugar together.
ADD remaining ingredients, mixing until smooth.
SPREAD chocolate filling on bottom cake layer.
COVER with top cake layer.
Hazelnut cream:
BEAT whipping cream to soft peaks. Gradually add icing sugar, vanilla sugar and Whip it, beating to stiff peaks.
FOLD hazelnuts into cream mixture gently.
SPREAD ⅔ of hazelnut cream over top and sides of cake.
DECORATE cake attractively with remaining hazelnut cream filling and chocolate leaves.

Chocolate Cream Torte

Batter:

4	egg yolks	4	
100 g	sugar	½	cup
1 pkg	**oetker** vanilla sugar	1	pkg.
1 btl	**oetker** rum flavouring concentrate	1	btl.
4	egg whites	4	
100 g	all-purpose flour	⅔	cup
4 g	**oetker** baking powder	1	tsp.
50 g	ground hazelnuts or walnuts	½	cup

Filling:

75 mL	coffee cream	5	tbsp.
6 sq	semi-sweet chocolate	6	sq.
70 g	sugar	⅓	cup
1 pkg	**oetker** vanilla sugar	1	pkg.
1 btl	**oetker** rum flavouring concentrate	1	btl.
1	egg yolk	1	
250 mL	whipping cream	1	cup
2 pkg	**oetker** Whip it	2	pkg.

Batter:
PREHEAT oven to 180°C (350°F). Grease 24 cm (9½") spring form pan. Line with waxed paper.
COMBINE egg yolks, ⅔ of sugar, vanilla sugar and rum flavouring in mixer bowl. Beat at high speed of electric mixer until thick and creamy.
BEAT egg whites and remaining sugar to stiff peaks.
FOLD into egg yolk mixture.
SIFT flour, baking powder and ground nuts together over egg mixture. Fold in gently.
TURN batter into prepared pan.
BAKE on lower oven rack at 180°C (350°F) for 35-40 minutes or until toothpick inserted in centre comes out clean.
REMOVE from pan immediately. Remove waxed paper and let cake cool completely.
SLICE cake horizontally with thread to make 2 layers.
Filling:
COMBINE coffee cream, chocolate and sugar. Heat gently to a boil, stirring constantly.
REMOVE from heat.
ADD vanilla sugar, rum flavouring and egg yolk.

18

Chocolate Cream Torte (cont.)

Decoration:

100 g	chocolate sprinkles	1 cup
	candied flowers, optional	

BLEND smoothly. Cool.
BEAT whipping cream to soft peaks. Gradually add Whip it, beating to stiff peaks.
FOLD into chocolate cream gently.
SPREAD bottom layer of cake with ⅔ of chocolate cream mixture.
COVER with top cake layer.
SPREAD remaining chocolate cream mixture over top and sides of cake.
COVER sides with chocolate sprinkles.
DECORATE with candied flowers, if desired.

Recipe No. 103

Lucullus Almond Wine Torte

Batter:

6	egg yolks	6
200 g	sugar	1 cup
60 mL	orange juice	4 tbsp.
1 btl	**oetker** rum flavouring concentrate	1 btl.
1 pkg	**oetker** vanilla sugar	1 pkg.
6	egg whites	6
100 g	all-purpose flour	⅔ cup
8 g	**oetker** baking powder	2 tsp.
300 g	ground almonds	3 cups

Filling:

1 pkg	**oetker** vanilla pudding mix	1 pkg.
150 g	sugar	¾ cup
500 mL	white wine	2 cups
200 g	sweet (unsalted) butter	1 cup
10 drops	**oetker** lemon flavouring concentrate	10 drops
15 mL	apricot jam	1 tbsp.
250 mL	whipping cream	1 cup
1 pkg	**oetker** Whip it	1 pkg.
60 mL	apricot jam	4 tbsp.
30 mL	rum	2 tbsp.

Decoration:

100 g	toasted sliced almonds	1 cup
	chocolate decorations, optional	

Batter:
PREHEAT oven to 180°C (350°F). Grease a 26 cm (10½") spring form pan. Line with waxed paper
COMBINE egg yolks, ⅔ of sugar, orange juice, and rum flavouring in mixer bowl. Beat at high speed until thick and creamy.
BEAT egg whites and remaining sugar to stiff peaks.
MIX flour, baking powder and ground almonds together. Fold into egg yolk mixture gently but thoroughly.
FOLD egg whites into egg yolk mixture gently.
TURN into prepared pan.
BAKE on lower oven rack at 180°C (350°F) for 40-50 minutes or until toothpick inserted in centre comes out clean.
REMOVE from pan immediately. Remove waxed paper and let cake cool completely.
CUT cake horizontally with thread to make 2 layers.
Filling:
COMBINE vanilla pudding mix, sugar and 125 mL (½ cup) wine in small bowl. Stir until smoothly blended.
HEAT remaining wine in saucepan to boiling. Stir in pudding mixture. Bring to boil again, stirring constantly.
REMOVE from heat. Cool to room temperature, stirring occasionally.
CREAM butter. Beat in pudding, one spoonful at a time. (Butter and pudding must be at same temperature to prevent curdling).
ADD lemon flavouring and 15 mL (1 tbsp.) jam.
MIX until smoothly blended.
BEAT whipping cream. Gradually add Whip it, beating to stiff peaks.
FOLD into wine cream.
MIX remaining 60 mL (4 tbsp.) apricot jam with rum.
SPREAD ½ of the jam mixture over bottom layer of cake. Cover with ⅔ of the cream filling.
PLACE top cake layer over cream filling.
SPREAD remaining jam on top and sides of cake. Cover with remaining cream.
SPRINKLE sides with toasted sliced almonds and decorate top with chocolate if desired.

Poppy Seed Apricot Torte

Batter:

100 g	chopped dried apricots	¾	cup
45 mL	apricot brandy	3	tbsp.
6	eggs	6	
200 g	sugar	1	cup
1 pkg	**oetker** vanilla sugar	1	pkg.
pinch	ground cloves		pinch
pinch	cinnamon		pinch
2 drops	**oetker** lemon flavouring concentrate	2	drops
150 g	ground poppy seeds	1	cup
120 g	all-purpose flour	¾	cup
8 g	**oetker** baking powder	2	tsp.

Filling:

250 mL	whipping cream	1	cup
1 pkg	**oetker** Whip it	1	pkg.
1 pkg	**oetker** vanilla sugar	1	pkg.
30 mL	apricot brandy	2	tbsp.
30 mL	apricot jam	2	tbsp.
6	canned apricot halves, chopped	6	

Decoration:

10	apricot halves	10	
4 sq	semi-sweet chocolate, grated	4	sq.

Batter:
SOAK chopped dried apricots in apricot brandy.
PREHEAT oven to 180°C (350°F). Grease a 26 cm (10½") spring form pan. Line with waxed paper.
COMBINE eggs, sugar, vanilla sugar, cloves, cinnamon and lemon flavouring in mixer bowl.
BEAT at high speed of electric mixer until thick and creamy.
STIR poppy seeds into creamed mixture.
SIFT flour and baking powder together. Fold in gently.
FOLD in apricots.
TURN batter into prepared pan.
BAKE on lower oven rack at 180°C (350°F) for 45-55 minutes or until toothpick inserted in centre comes out clean.
REMOVE from pan immediately. Remove waxed paper and let cake cool completely.
SLICE cake in half horizontally with thread to make 2 layers.
Filling:
BEAT whipping cream to soft peaks. Gradually add Whip it and vanilla sugar, beating to stiff peaks.
FOLD in apricot brandy and apricot jam.
SPREAD ⅓ of filling on bottom cake layer.
SPREAD chopped apricots over cream.
COVER with top cake layer.
SPREAD sides and top of cake evenly with part of remaining filling.
COVER sides of cake with grated chocolate.
DECORATE cake attractively with remaining filling and apricot halves.

Apricot Cake

Batter:

150 g	butter or margarine	¾	cup
150 g	sugar	¾	cup
1 pkg	**oetker** vanilla sugar	1	pkg.
3	eggs	3	
6 drops	**oetker** lemon flavouring concentrate	6	drops
45 mL	apricot brandy	3	tbsp.
200 g	all-purpose flour	1¼	cups
4 g	**oetker** baking powder	1	tsp.
pinch	cinnamon		pinch

Filling:

500-600 g	fresh or canned apricot halves	1-1½	lbs.
30 mL	strained apricot jam	2	tbsp.
45 mL	apricot brandy	3	tbsp.

Batter:
PREHEAT oven to 180°C (350°F). Grease and flour bottom of 26 cm (10½") spring form pan.
CREAM butter, sugar and vanilla sugar together in mixer bowl.
BEAT in eggs, one at a time, lemon flavouring and apricot brandy, beating until light and fluffy.
SIFT flour, baking powder and cinnamon together. Gradually beat into creamed mixture.
TURN batter into prepared pan.
Filling:
COVER batter with apricot halves, reserving some for garnish.
BAKE on lower oven rack at 180°C (350°F) for 50-60 minutes or until toothpick inserted in centre comes out clean.
COMBINE apricot jam and apricot brandy. Mix well.
SPREAD mixture evenly over cake immediately after baking.
COOL cake in pan for 10 minutes, then remove and let cool completely.
DECORATE with reserved apricots.
SPRINKLE with sugar before serving.

Chocolate Orange Torte

Batter:

150	g	butter	¾ cup
150	g	sugar	¾ cup
1	pkg	**oetker** vanilla sugar	1 pkg.
3		eggs	3
200	g	all-purpose flour	1¼ cups
4	g	**oetker** baking powder	1 tsp.
100	g	ground almonds	1 cup
4	sq	semi-sweet chocolate, chopped	4 sq.
125	mL	orange juice	½ cup

Filling:

125	mL	orange marmalade	½ cup

Glaze:

1	pkg	**oetker** Chocofix	1 pkg.

Batter:
PREHEAT oven to 180°C (350°F). Grease and flour bottom of 24 cm (9½") spring form pan.
CREAM butter, sugar and vanilla sugar together.
BEAT in eggs, one at a time, beating until light and fluffy.
COMBINE flour, baking powder, ground almonds and chopped chocolate. Mix well.
FOLD into creamed mixture alternately with orange juice, mixing thoroughly.
TURN batter into prepared pan.
BAKE on lower oven rack at 180°C (350°F) for 50-60 min.
REMOVE from pan immediately and cool completely.
Filling and Glaze:
SPREAD top and sides of cake with marmalade.
PREPARE Chocofix according to package directions.
COVER cake with chocolate glaze. Let set before decorating.
Decoration:
Decorate attractively with whipped cream and whole almonds.

Orange Cream Torte

Batter:

6		egg yolks	6
150	g	sugar	¾ cup
1	pkg	**oetker** vanilla sugar	1 pkg.
1	btl	**oetker** lemon flavouring concentrate	1 btl.
6		egg whites	6
110	g	all-purpose flour	¾ cup
4	g	**oetker** baking powder	1 tsp.
2	sq	semi-sweet chocolate, grated	2 sq.
30	g	ground almonds	⅓ cup

Filling:

1	pkg	**oetker** vanilla pudding	1 pkg.
150	g	sugar	¾ cup
200	mL	milk	¾ cup
250	mL	orange juice	1 cup
15	mL	lemon juice	1 tbsp.
200	g	sweet (unsalted) butter	1 cup
10	mL	grated orange rind	2 tsp.
45	mL	apricot brandy	3 tbsp.
30	mL	orange juice	2 tbsp.

Decoration:

4	sq	semi-sweet chocolate, shaved	4 sq.
		orange slices	

Batter:
PREHEAT oven to 180°C (350°F). Grease and flour bottom of 24 cm (9½") spring form pan.
COMBINE egg yolks, ⅔ of sugar, vanilla sugar and lemon flavouring in mixer bowl.
BEAT at high speed of mixer until thick and creamy.
BEAT egg whites and remaining sugar to stiff peaks.
SIFT flour and baking powder together over egg yolk mixture. Add grated chocolate and almonds. Fold in gently but thoroughly.
FOLD egg whites gently into egg yolk mixture.
TURN into prepared pan.
BAKE on lower oven rack at 180°C (350°F) for 40-45 minutes.
REMOVE from pan immediately and let cake cool.
SLICE cake horizontally with thread to make 2 layers.
Filling:
COMBINE vanilla pudding mix, sugar and milk in small bowl and stir until smoothly blended.
HEAT orange and lemon juice to boiling.
STIR in pudding mixture. Bring to a boil, stirring constantly.
REMOVE from heat. Cool to room temperature, stirring occasionally.
CREAM butter. Beat in pudding a spoonful at a time. (Butter and pudding must be at same temperature to prevent curdling).
FOLD grated orange rind into mixture.
SPRINKLE bottom cake layer with some of apricot brandy and orange juice.
SPREAD bottom with ⅔ of filling.
COVER with orange pieces.
PLACE second cake layer on top.
SPRINKLE with apricot brandy and orange juice.
SPREAD top and sides with cream filling.
DECORATE with shaved chocolate and orange slices.

Continued on page 26.

24

Kiwi Torte

Batter:

150 g	sweet (unsalted) butter	¾	cup
150 g	sugar	¾	cup
1 pkg	**oetker** vanilla sugar	1	pkg.
3	eggs	3	
15 mL	lemon juice	1	tbsp.
100 mL	orange juice	7	tbsp.
200 g	all-purpose four	1¼	cups
4 g	**oetker** baking powder	1	tsp.
50 g	ground almonds	½	cup

Filling:

50 mL	apricot jam or marmalade	¼	cup

Topping:

3	kiwi fruits	3	
1 can	mandarin orange sections, drained	1	can
250 mL	whipping cream	1	cup
1 pkg	**oetker** Whip it	1	pkg.
1 pkg	**oetker** vanilla sugar	1	pkg.
50 mL	apricot jam or marmalade	¼	cup

Decoration:

50 g	toasted, sliced almonds	½	cup

Batter:
PREHEAT oven to 180°C (350°F). Grease and flour bottom of 26 cm (10½″) spring form pan.
CREAM butter, sugar and vanilla sugar in mixer bowl.
BEAT in eggs, one at a time, lemon juice and orange juice, beating until light and fluffy.
COMBINE flour, baking powder and ground almonds; mix well. Gradually add to creamed mixture.
TURN batter into prepared pan.
BAKE on lower oven rack at 180°C (350°F) for 35-45 minutes or until toothpick inserted in centre comes out clean.
REMOVE from pan immediately and let cake cool completely.
SLICE cake horizontally with thread to make 2 layers.
Filling & Topping:
SPREAD 50 mL (¼ cup) jam between cake layers.
PEEL and slice kiwis.
DRAIN mandarin oranges.
BEAT whipping cream in small bowl to soft peaks. Gradually add Whip it and vanilla sugar, beating to stiff peaks.
SPREAD jam over top and sides of cake.
SPRINKLE sides with toasted, sliced almonds.
DECORATE top of cake in circular fashion with halved kiwi slices and mandarins.
DECORATE spaces between fruit attractively with whipped cream.

Filled Nut Torte

Batter:

150 g	sweet (unsalted) butter	¾	cup
150 g	sugar	¾	cup
1 pkg	**oetker** vanilla sugar	1	pkg.
3	eggs	3	
75 mL	rum	5	tbsp.
45 mL	lemon juice	3	tbsp.
200 g	all-purpose flour	1¼	cups
4 g	**oetker** baking powder	1	tsp.
5 mL	cinnamon	1	tsp.

Filling:

100 g	ground almonds	1	cup
30 g	ground pistachios	⅓	cup
30 g	sugar	1	oz.
5 mL	cinnamon	1	tsp.

Glaze:

250 g	sifted icing sugar	1⅔	cups
30 mL	lemon juice	2	tbsp.
15-30 mL	hot water	1-2	tbsp.

Batter:
PREHEAT oven to 230°C (450°F). Grease and flour bottom of a 26 cm (10½″) spring form pan.
CREAM butter, sugar and vanilla sugar together in mixer bowl.
BEAT in eggs, one at a time, rum and lemon juice, beating until light and fluffy.
SIFT flour, baking powder and cinnamon together. Gradually beat into creamed mixture.
Filling:
COMBINE almonds, pistachios, sugar and cinnamon.
COVER bottom of spring form pan with 45-60 mL (3-4 tbsp.) of batter.
SPRINKLE lightly with some nut mixture.
BAKE for 4-5 minutes at 230°C (450°F) until golden brown.
SPREAD 45-60 mL (3-4 tbsp.) batter over baked layer.
SPRINKLE lightly with nut mixture.
BAKE for 4-5 minutes at 230°C (450°F) until golden brown.
REPEAT above until all batter and nut filling is used up.
REMOVE from pan immediately and let cake cool completely.

Continued on page 28.

Filled Nut Torte (cont.)

Decoration:
    maraschino cherries
    ground pistachios

Glaze:
COMBINE sifted icing sugar, lemon juice and hot water.
STIR till smooth and of glaze consistency.
COVER top and sides of cake with glaze.
DECORATE attractively with maraschino cherries and pistachios.

Recipe No. 110

Lemon Cream Torte

Batter:

150 g	sweet (unsalted) butter	¾	cup
150 g	sugar	¾	cup
1 pkg	**oetker** vanilla sugar	1	pkg.
5	egg yolks	5	
45 mL	lemon juice	3	tbsp.
1 btl	**oetker** lemon flavouring concentrate	1	btl.
3 drops	**oetker** almond flavouring concentrate	3	drops
250 g	all-purpose flour	1¾	cups
1 pkg	**oetker** baking powder (14 g/1 tbsp.)	1	pkg.
5	egg whites	5	

Filling:

1 pkg	**oetker** vanilla pudding mix	1	pkg.
150 g	sugar	¾	cup
500 mL	milk	2	cups
45 mL	lemon juice	3	tbsp.
30 mL	apricot brandy	2	tbsp.
250 g	sweet (unsalted) butter	1	cup
125 mL	apricot jam or marmalade	½	cup

Decoration:

100 g	sugar sprinkles	½	cup
	lemon slices		
	sugar flowers		

Batter:
PREHEAT oven to 180°C (350°F). Grease and flour a 26 cm (10½") spring form pan.
CREAM butter and gradually add sugar, vanilla sugar, egg yolks, apricot jam, lemon and almond flavourings, beating until light and fluffy.
SIFT flour, baking powder and nutmeg together. Add to creamed mixture gradually.
BEAT egg whites to stiff peaks. Fold into batter gently.
TURN batter into prepared pan.
BAKE on middle oven rack at 180°C (350°F) for 40-50 minutes or until toothpick inserted in centre comes out clean.
REMOVE from pan immediately and let cake cool completely.
CUT cake with thread horizontally into 3 even layers.

Filling:
COMBINE vanilla pudding mix and 125 mL (½ cup) milk in small bowl. Stir until smooth. Rinse saucepan with cold water.
HEAT remaining 375 mL (1½ cups) milk to boiling. Stir in pudding mixture. Bring to a boil, stirring constantly.
REMOVE from heat. Cool to room temperature, stirring occasionally.
ADD lemon juice and apricot brandy.
CREAM butter. Beat in pudding a spoonful at a time. (Butter and pudding must be at same temperature to prevent curdling).
COVER bottom cake layer with some of jam.
SPREAD ⅓ of the cream filling over jam.
PLACE second cake layer over filling. Press down gently but firmly.
COVER layer with jam.
SPREAD ⅓ of cream filling over jam.
PLACE top layer over filling.
SPREAD top and sides of cake with jam.
COVER with cream filling reserving a little for decoration.
COVER sides with sugar sprinkles.
DECORATE cake attractively with the remaining cream, lemon slices and sugar flowers.

Recipe No. 111

Raspberry Marzipan Torte

Batter:

6	eggs	6
240 g	sugar	1¼ cups
1 pkg	**oetker** vanilla sugar	1 pkg.
100 g	all-purpose flour	⅔ cup
4 g	**oetker** baking powder	1 tsp.
5 g	cocoa	1 tsp.
100 g	ground walnuts or hazelnuts	1 cup

Paris Cream:

250 mL	whipping cream	1 cup
10 sq	semi-sweet chocolate, chopped	10 sq.

Filling:

45 mL	raspberry jam	3 tbsp
150 g	almond paste	5 oz.
100 g	icing sugar	¾ cup
15 mL	rum	1 tbsp.
500 g	fresh or frozen raspberries	1 lb.

Glaze:

1 pkg	**oetker** red cake glaze	1 pkg.
250 mL	water or fruit juice	1 cup

Decoration:

250 mL	whipping cream	1 cup
1 pkg	**oetker** Whip it	1 pkg.

Batter:
PREHEAT oven to 180°C (350°F). Grease a 26 cm (10½") spring form pan. Line with waxed paper.
COMBINE eggs, sugar and vanilla sugar.
BEAT at high speed of electric mixer until creamy.
STIR flour, baking powder, cocoa and ground nuts together. Fold into egg mixture gently.
TURN batter into prepared pan.
BAKE on lower oven rack at 180°C (350°F) for 45-50 minutes.
REMOVE from pan immediately and let cake cool completely.
SLICE cake in half horizontally with thread.
Paris Cream and Filling:
COMBINE chopped chocolate and whipping cream in saucepan. Bring slowly to a boil, stirring constantly. Let cool.
BEAT with electric mixer until smooth and creamy.
SPREAD ⅔ of cream filling on bottom cake layer.
PLACE top cake layer over filling. Spread jam on top cake layer.
KNEAD almond paste, icing sugar and rum together to a smooth paste.
ROLL out to a circle the size of top cake layer.
PLACE on top cake layer.
COVER with raspberries.
PLACE ring of spring form pan around cake.
PREPARE glaze according to directions on package.
SPOON evenly over raspberries. Let set.
REMOVE ring of spring form pan.
SPREAD remaining chocolate cream filling on sides of cake.
BEAT whipping cream and Whip it to stiff peaks. Decorate top edge of torte attractively.

Recipe No. 112

Fruit Torte

Batter:

100 g	sweet (unsalted) butter	½ cup
100 g	sugar	½ cup
1 pkg	**oetker** vanilla sugar	1 pkg.
3	eggs	3
1 btl	**oetker** lemon flavouring concentrate	1 btl.
150 g	all-purpose flour	1 cup
4 g	**oetker** baking powder	1 tsp.
50 mL	milk	¼ cup

Filling:

45 mL	apricot jam	3 tbsp.
500-750 g	fresh or canned fruit (kiwi, pineapple, strawberries, grapes, mandarins, apricots etc.)	1-1½ lbs.

Glaze:

1 pkg	**oetker** clear cake glaze	1 pkg.
250 mL	water, fruit juice or wine	1 cup

Batter:
PREHEAT oven to 180°C (350°F). Lightly grease and flour a 2 L (39 cm × 26 cm/15″ × 10″) jelly roll pan.
BEAT butter at high speed of electric mixer until thick and creamy. Gradually add all ingredients. Mix well.
SPREAD batter evenly in prepared pan.
BAKE on middle oven rack at 180°C (350°F) for 30-40 minutes or until toothpick inserted in centre comes out clean.
REMOVE from pan immediately. Place a cold wet cloth on back of pan for easy removal of cake. Cool cake completely.
Filling:
SPREAD top of cake with jam.
ARRANGE fruit attractively over jam.
PREPARE glaze according to directions on package.
SPOON evenly over fruit. Let set.

Poppy Seed Slices

Pastry:

180 g	flour	1¼ cups	
4 g	**oetker** baking powder	1 tsp.	
60 g	sugar	⅓ cup	
1 pkg	**oetker** vanilla sugar	1 pkg.	
1	egg	1	
125 g	sweet (unsalted) COLD butter	½ cup	

Filling:

250 mL	milk	1 cup	
200 g	sugar	1 cup	
1 pkg	**oetker** vanilla sugar	1 pkg.	
30 mL	honey	2 tbsp.	
350 g	ground poppy seeds	2⅓ cups	
½ btl	**oetker** rum flavouring concentrate	½ btl.	
1 dash	cinnamon	1 dash	
30 g	raisins	¼ cup	

Pastry:
PREHEAT oven to 180°C (350°F). Grease a 25 cm × 30 cm (10″ × 12″) cake pan.
SIFT flour and baking powder together onto pastry board. Make a well in centre.
PLACE sugar, vanilla sugar and egg in well.
WORK a little flour into centre ingredients to make a thick paste.
CUT cold butter into small pieces over flour mixture. Working quickly from the centre, work all ingredients together to make a smooth dough. If dough is sticky, chill slightly for easy handling.
PRESS or roll ½ of dough onto prepared pan.
Filling:
COMBINE milk, sugar, vanilla sugar, honey and poppy seeds in saucepan. Bring to a boil, stirring constantly. Add rum flavouring, cinnamon and raisins. Let cool.
SPREAD evenly on pastry.
ROLL out remaining dough to size of pan.
COVER poppy seed mixture with second pastry layer. With fork make several holes in pastry.
BAKE on middle oven rack at 180°C (350°F) for 30-45 minutes or until golden.
BRUSH top layer with melted butter just a few minutes before done. Cool. Cut into slices.
SPRINKLE with icing sugar, if desired.

Walnut Rum Squares

Batter:

6	egg yolks	6	
120 g	sugar	¾ cup	
1 pkg	**oetker** vanilla sugar	1 pkg.	
10 drops	**oetker** lemon flavouring concentrate	10 drops	
6	egg whites	6	
180 g	all-purpose flour	1¼ cups	
1 g	**oetker** baking powder	¼ tsp.	

Filling:

15 mL	lemon juice	1 tbsp.	
60 mL	orange juice	4 tbsp.	
120 mL	rum	8 tbsp.	
50 g	sugar	¼ cup	
100 g	dry bread crumbs	1 cup	
1 pkg	**oetker** vanilla sugar	1 pkg.	
90 mL	apricot jam or marmalade	6 tbsp.	
20 g	cocoa	2 tbsp.	
250 g	ground walnuts	2½ cups	

Batter:
PREHEAT oven to 180°C (350°F). Grease and line a 2 L (39 cm × 26 cm/15″ × 10″) jelly roll pan with waxed paper. Grease again and dust lightly with flour.
COMBINE egg yolks, ⅔ of sugar, vanilla sugar and lemon flavouring in mixer bowl. Beat at high speed of electric mixer until thick and creamy.
BEAT egg whites and remaining sugar to stiff peaks. Fold into egg yolk mixture gently.
SIFT flour and baking powder over egg mixture and fold in gently but thoroughly.
SPREAD batter evenly in prepared pan.
BAKE on middle oven rack at 180°C (350°F) for 10-15 minutes or until golden.
TURN out immediately onto waxed paper sprinkled with sugar. Remove waxed paper gently from back of cake. Place a cold wet cloth on waxed paper if necessary for easy removal.
LET cool completely.
CUT cake into 2 equal pieces.
Filling:
COMBINE lemon juice, orange juice, rum, sugar and bread crumbs in saucepan. Bring to a boil, stirring constantly.
STIR in vanilla sugar, jam, cocoa and ground walnuts.

Continued on page 34.

Walnut Rum Squares (cont.)

Glaze:

150 g	sifted icing sugar	1 cup
1 btl	**oetker** run flavouring concentrate	1 btl.
15-30 mL	hot water	1-2 tbsp.

Topping:

30 mL	redcurrant jam or marmalade	2 tbsp.

Decoration:

maraschino cherries

Glaze:
BEAT sifted icing sugar, rum flavouring and hot water together to a smooth glaze consistency.
SPREAD top layer with jam and cover with glaze.
CUT into desired squares.
DECORATE each square with a maraschino cherry.

Marzipan Filled Jelly Roll

Batter:

4	egg yolks	4
100 g	sugar	½ cup
1 pkg	**oetker** vanilla sugar	1 pkg.
4	egg whites	4
100 g	all-purpose flour	⅔ cup
1 g	**oetker** baking powder	¼ tsp.

Filling:

1 pkg	**oetker** vanilla pudding mix	1 pkg.
500 mL	milk	2 cups
175 g	sugar	¾ cup
1 btl	**oetker** rum flavouring concentrate	1 btl.
5 drops	**oetker** lemon flavouring concentrate	5 drops
3 drops	**oetker** almond flavouring concentrate	3 drops
200 g	sweet (unsalted) butter	1 cup
75 mL	apricot jam or marmalade	⅓ cup

Decoration:

400 g	almond paste	14 oz.
200 g	icing sugar	1⅓ cups
1 pkg	**oetker** Chocofix	1 pkg.

Batter:
PREHEAT oven to 180°C (350°F). Grease a 2 L (39 cm × 26 cm/15" × 10") jelly roll pan and line with waxed paper. Grease again.
COMBINE egg yolks, ⅔ of sugar and vanilla sugar in mixer bowl. Beat at high speed of electric mixer until thick and creamy.
SIFT flour and baking powder together over egg yolk mixture. Fold in gently but thoroughly.
BEAT egg whites and remaining ⅓ of sugar to stiff peaks. FOLD egg whites into egg yolk mixture gently.
SPREAD batter evenly in prepared pan.
BAKE on middle oven rack at 180°C (350°F) for 10-12 minutes or until toothpick inserted in centre comes out clean.
TURN out immediately onto tea towel sprinkled with sugar. Remove waxed paper. Place a cold wet cloth, on waxed paper if necessary for easy removal.
ROLL up cake in towel immediately, starting at narrow edge. Let cake cool completely in towel.
Filling:
COMBINE vanilla pudding mix, 125 mL (½ cup) milk, sugar, lemon, rum and almond flavourings in small bowl. Stir until smoothly blended.
HEAT remaining 375 mL (1½ cups) milk to boiling. Stir in pudding mixture. Bring to a boil, stirring constantly.
REMOVE from heat. Cool to room temperature, stirring occasionally.
CREAM butter. Beat in pudding one spoonful at a time. (Butter and pudding must be at same temperature to prevent curdling).
UNROLL cake.
SPREAD thinly with some of the apricot jam.
FILL pudding into decorating bag without spout.
FILL middle of cake with thick roll of pudding mixture.
ROLL cake up again. Cool.
KNEAD almond paste and icing sugar together to a smooth paste. Roll out thinly.
SPREAD remaining jam over top and sides of cake.
ROLL almond paste layer around cake.
Decoration:
SOFTEN Chocofix in boiling water according to package directions. Drizzle chocolate over cake.

Apple Meringue Squares

Batter:

150 g	sweet (unsalted) butter	¾	cup
150 g	sugar	¾	cup
1 pkg	**oetker** vanilla sugar	1	pkg.
3	eggs	3	
1 btl	**oetker** lemon flavouring concentrate	1	btl.
300 g	all-purpose flour	2	cups
1 pkg	**oetker** baking powder (14 g/1 tbsp)	1	pkg.
1 pinch	cinnamon	1	pinch

Filling:

1 kg	apples	2	lbs.
2	egg yolks	2	
100 g	sugar	½	cup
1 pkg	**oetker** vanilla sugar	1	pkg.
30 mL	lemon juice	2	tbsp.
45 mL	apricot jam or marmalade	3	tbsp.
100 g	ground almonds	1	cup
50 g	raisins	½	cup

Meringue:

2	egg whites	2	
100 g	sugar	½	cup

Batter:
PREHEAT oven to 200°C (400°F). Grease and flour a 3.5 L (33 cm × 23 cm/13″ × 9″) cake pan.
CREAM butter, sugar, vanilla sugar, eggs and lemon flavouring together until light and fluffy.
SIFT flour, baking powder and cinnamon together over creamed mixture. Stir well to blend.
TURN batter into prepared pan.
Filling:
PEEL and core apples. Cut into thin slices.
CREAM egg yolks, sugar, vanilla sugar, lemon juice and jam together.
FOLD in almonds, raisins and apples (gently but thoroughly).
SPREAD mixture evenly over batter.
BAKE on middle oven rack at 200°C (400°F) for 35-40 minutes or until set.
Meringue:
BEAT egg whites to soft peaks. Gradually add sugar, beating to stiff peaks.
FILL into pastry bag with star tip. Pipe onto prebaked cake in criss-cross pattern.
BAKE at 200°C (400°F) for 5 more minutes or until golden.
COOL. Cut cake into desired size squares.

Blueberry Cream Cheese Diamonds

Batter:

5	egg yolks	5	
150 g	sugar	¾	cup
1 pkg	**oetker** vanilla sugar	1	pkg.
1 btl	**oetker** lemon flavouring concentrate	1	btl.
110 g	all-purpose flour	¾	cup
1 g	**oetker** baking powder	¼	tsp.
5	egg whites	5	

Filling:

1 pkg	**oetker** cheesecake filling mix	1	pkg.
500 mL	water	2	cups
500 g	strained quark, ricotta or cream cheese	2	cups
250 mL	whipping cream	1	cup
45 mL	red currant jam or marmalade	3	tbsp.

Blueberry Mousse:

500 g	fresh or frozen blueberries	1	lb.
250 mL	whipping cream	1	cup
1 pkg	**oetker** Whip-it	1	pkg.
2 pkgs	**oetker** vanilla sugar	2	pkgs.

Batter:
PREHEAT oven to 180°C (350°F). Grease a 2 L (39 cm × 26 cm/15″ × 10″) jelly roll pan and line with waxed paper. Grease again.
COMBINE egg yolks, sugar, vanilla sugar and lemon flavouring in mixer bowl. Beat at high speed of electric mixer until thick and creamy.
SIFT flour and baking powder together over egg yolk mixture and fold in gently.
BEAT egg whites to stiff peaks. Fold gently into egg yolk mixture.
TURN batter into prepared pan, spreading evenly.
BAKE on middle oven rack at 180°C (350°F) for 20-25 minutes or until toothpick inserted in centre comes out clean.
REMOVE from pan immediately. Remove waxed paper and let cake cool completely.
Filling:
COMBINE cheesecake filling mix and water. Beat until foamy.
BEAT quark or cheese until smooth. Gradually add to prepared filling mixture.
BEAT whipping cream to stiff peaks. Fold into cheese mixture.
SPREAD jam on cake.
COVER evenly with cheese mixture. Cool.
CUT into diamond shaped slices.
PURÉE blueberries.
BEAT whipping cream to soft peaks. Gradually add Whip-it and vanilla sugar. Continue beating until stiff. Fold blueberry purée into cream mixture.
DECORATE squares attractively with blueberry cream.

Black Forest Jelly Roll

Batter:

5	egg yolks	5
100 g	sugar	½ cup
1 pkg	**oetker** vanilla sugar	1 pkg.
120 g	all-purpose flour	¾ cup
pinch	**oetker** baking powder	pinch
5	egg whites	5

Filling:

1 pkg	**oetker** vanilla pudding mix	1 pkg.
150 g	sugar	¾ cup
500 mL	milk	2 cups
30 mL	lemon juice	1 tbsp.
45 mL	cherry juice	3 tbsp.
200 g	sweet (unsalted) butter	1 cup
200 g	cherry pie filling	1 cup

Decoration:

2 sq	semi-sweet chocolate, shaved	2 sq.
	cherries	

Batter:
PREHEAT oven to 180°C (350°F). Grease a 2 L (39 cm × 26 cm/15″ × 10″) jelly roll pan and line with waxed paper. Grease again.
COMBINE egg yolks, ⅔ of sugar and vanilla sugar in mixer bowl. Beat at high speed of electric mixer until thick and creamy.
SIFT flour and baking powder together over egg yolk mixture and fold in gently.
BEAT egg whites and remaining ⅓ of sugar to stiff peaks. Fold gently into yolk mixture.
SPREAD batter evenly in prepared pan.
BAKE on middle oven rack at 180°C (350°F) for 10-12 minutes or until toothpick inserted in centre comes out clean.
TURN out immediately onto tea towel sprinkled with sugar. Remove waxed paper off cake back. Rub paper with a cool wet cloth, if necessary for easy removal.
ROLL UP cake in towel immediately, starting at narrow edge.
Let cake cool completely in towel.

Filling:
COMBINE vanilla pudding mix, sugar and 125 mL (½ cup) milk in small bowl. Stir until smooth blended.
RINSE saucepan with cold water.
HEAT remaining 375 mL (1½ cups) milk to boiling.
STIR in pudding mixture. Bring to a boil stirring constantly.
REMOVE from heat.
STIR in lemon juice and cherry juice.
COOL to room temperature, stirring occasionally.
CREAM butter. Beat in pudding one spoonful at a time. (Butter and pudding must be at same temperature to prevent curdling).
FOLD cherry pie filling into cream mixture.
UNROLL cake.
SPREAD ½ of filling evenly over cake and roll up again.
SPREAD ⅔ of remaining filling over top and sides (not ends) of cake.

Decoration:
SPRINKLE with shaved chocolate and decorate attractively with remaining filling and cherries.

Chestnut Cream Squares

Batter:

7	egg yolks	7
150 g	sugar	¾ cup
1 pkg	**oetker** vanilla sugar	1 pkg.
1 btl	**oetker** lemon flavouring concentrate	1 btl.
7	egg whites	7
50 g	all-purpose flour	⅓ cup
4 g	**oetker** baking powder	1 tsp.
150 g	ground walnuts	1½ cups
50 g	dry bread crumbs	½ cup

Paris Cream:

250 mL	whipping cream	1 cup
10 sq	semi-sweet chocolate, chopped	10 sq.

Chestnut Cream:

125 mL	whipping cream	½ cup
120 g	sugar	⅔ cup
1 pkg	**oetker** vanilla sugar	1 pkg.
½ pkg	**oetker** Whip-it	½ pkg.
1 btl	**oetker** rum flavouring concentrate	1 pkg.
200 g	chestnut purée, softened	7 oz.

Filling:

30 mL	red currant jam, raspberry jam or marmalade	2 tbsp.

Batter:
PREHEAT oven to 180°C (350°F). Grease a 2 L (39 cm × 26 cm/15″ × 10″) jelly roll pan.
SPRINKLE lightly with bread crumbs.
COMBINE egg yolks, ⅔ of sugar, vanilla sugar and lemon flavouring in mixer bowl. Beat at high speed of electric mixer until thick and creamy.
BEAT egg whites and remaining sugar to stiff peaks.
STIR flour, baking powder, ground walnuts and bread crumbs together. Fold into egg mixture gently.
FOLD in egg whites gently.
TURN batter into prepared pan spreading evenly.
BAKE at 180°C (350°F) on middle oven rack for 35-40 minutes or until toothpick inserted in centre comes out clean.
COOL cake completely.

Paris Cream:
COMBINE whipping cream and chocolate in saucepan. Bring to a boil, stirring constantly. Let cool.
BEAT with electric mixer until smooth and creamy.

Chestnut Cream:
BEAT whipping cream in mixer bowl to soft peaks.
Gradually add sugar, vanilla sugar, Whip-it and rum flavouring. Continue beating until stiff.
FOLD chestnut purée into cream mixture.
SPREAD jam on cake.
COVER evenly with Paris cream.
CUT into squares (approximately 6 cm × 6 cm/ 2½″ × 2½″).
DECORATE squares with rosettes of chestnut cream.

Coconut Almond Slices

Dough:

150 g	butter	¾	cup
120 g	sugar	⅔	cup
1 pkg	**oetker** vanilla sugar	1	pkg.
3	eggs	3	
1 btl	**oetker** lemon flavouring concentrate	1	btl.
500 g	all-purpose flour	3⅓	cups
250 mL	milk	1	cup

Topping:

250 g	raisins	2	cups
200 g	candied lemon & orange peel, chopped	1	cup
100 g	chopped almonds	⅔	cup
100 g	shredded coconut	1¼	cups
4 g	cinnamon	1	tsp.
80 g	sugar	⅓	cup
1 pkg	**oetker** vanilla sugar	1	pkg.
375 mL	whipping cream	1½	cups

Dough:
PREPARE topping and let stand while mixing dough.
PREHEAT oven to 200°C (400°F). Grease a 2 L (39 cm × 26 cm/15″ × 10″) jelly roll pan.
CREAM butter, sugar, vanilla sugar, eggs and lemon flavouring together in large mixer bowl.
SIFT flour and baking powder together. Gradually add to creamed mixture, alternating with just enough milk to make a stiff dough.
SPREAD dough evenly in prepared pan.

Topping:
COMBINE raisins, peel, almonds, coconut, cinnamon, sugar, vanilla sugar and whipping cream. Let stand for 30 minutes.
SPREAD mixture evenly over dough.
BAKE on middle oven rack at 200°C (400°F) for 30-40 minutes.
COOL and cut into slices.

Hazelnut Grape Slices

Batter:

150 g	butter	¾	cup
150 g	sugar	¾	cup
1 pkg	**oetker** vanilla sugar	1	pkg.
3	eggs	3	
6 drops	**oetker** lemon flavouring concentrate	6	drops
30 mL	apricot jam or marmalade	2	tbsp.
200 g	all-purpose flour	1¼	cups
4 g	**oetker** baking powder	1	tsp.
50 g	ground hazelnuts	½	cup
pinch	cinnamon		pinch

Topping:

500 mL	whipping cream	2	cups
2 pkgs	**oetker** Whip it	2	pkgs.
1 pkg	**oetker** vanilla sugar	1	pkg.
75 mL	apricot jam or marmalade	⅓	cup
500-750 g	green grapes	1-1½	lbs.

Batter:
PREHEAT oven to 180°C (350°F). Grease a 2 L (39 cm × 26 cm/15″ × 10″) jelly roll pan. Sprinkle lightly with bread crumbs.
CREAM butter, sugar and vanilla sugar together in mixer bowl.
BEAT in eggs, one at a time, lemon flavouring and apricot jam, beating until light and fluffy.
SIFT flour, baking powder, ground hazelnuts and cinnamon together. Gradually beat into creamed mixture.
SPREAD batter evenly in prepared pan.
BAKE on middle oven rack at 180°C (350°F) for 30-40 minutes or until toothpick inserted in centre comes out clean.
COOL cake completely.

Topping:
BEAT whipping cream to soft peaks. Gradually add Whip it and vanilla sugar. Continue beating until stiff.
SPREAD cake evenly with apricot jam.
DECORATE attractively, alternating a row of whipped cream (from decorator bag) and a row of grapes, covering cake completely.
CUT into serving slices.

Viennese Sour Cream Strudel

Dough:

250	g	all-purpose flour	1½	cups
15	mL	oil	1	tbsp.
	pinch	salt		pinch
1		egg	1	
125	mL	lukewarm water	½	cup

Filling:

6	slices	white bread	6	slices
250	mL	milk	1	cup
50	g	sweet (unsalted) butter	¼	cup
150	g	icing sugar, sifted	1	cup
1	pkg	**oetker** vanilla sugar	1	pkg.
4		egg yolks	4	
10	drops	**oetker** lemon flavouring concentrate	10	drops
	pinch	salt		pinch
250	mL	sour cream	1	cup
30	g	cream of wheat	¼	cup
150	g	raisins	1¼	cups
4		egg whites	4	
50	g	sweet (unsalted) butter, melted	¼	cup
500	mL	hot milk	2	cups
75	mL	sweet (unsalted) butter	⅓	cup

Vanilla Sauce:

750	mL	milk	3	cups
.100	g	sugar	½	cup
1	pkg	**oetker** vanilla pudding mix	1	pkg.
1		egg yolk	1	
2	pkg	**oetker** vanilla sugar	2	pkg.

Dough:

PREHEAT oven to 200°C (400°F). Grease a large baking pan.
SIFT flour onto pastry board. Make a well in centre.
PUT oil, salt, egg and water into well.
COMBINE ingredients mixing from centre with a fork to make a stiff dough. Work dough until smooth, shin and blistered in appearance.
SHAPE dough into a small loaf.
BRUSH lightly with oil.
COVER with a thick cloth and let rest in a warm plac for 1 hour.
PLACE a linen tablecloth over a large table. Sprinkle with flour.
ROLL dough thinly on cloth, then start to pull the dough to stretch it. Stretch dough by putting it over the back of your hands and gently pulling outward in all directions. Stretch dough as thin as possible.

Filling:

REMOVE bread crusts, cut bread into small pieces.
SOAK in 250 mL (1 cup) milk.
BEAT in gradually butter, icing sugar, vanilla sugar, egg yolks, lemon flavouring, salt, sour cream, cream o wheat and raisins.
BEAT egg whites to stiff peaks.
FOLD egg whites into raisin mixture.
BRUSH melted butter over dough.
SPREAD filling over ½ of dough.
ROLL up tightly starting at end with filling, using tablecloth to help you roll.
PLACE in greased baking pan.
BRUSH lightly with melted butter.
BAKE on lower oven rack at 200°C (400°F) for 40-45 minutes or until crisp and golden.
HEAT 500 mL milk.
ADD 75 mL (⅓ cup) butter.
After 15-20 minutes baking time:
SLOWLY pour hot milk/butter beside strudel into baking pan.

Vanilla Sauce:

PREPARE vanilla pudding mix according to direction on package using 750 mL (3 cups) milk and sugar to make a sauce consistency. Gradually stir egg yolk and vanilla sugar into mixture.
CUT strudel into serving pieces.
SERVE with vanilla sauce.

Glazed Apple Ring Cake

Batter:

150 g	butter	¾	cup
150 g	sugar	¾	cup
1 pkg	**oetker** vanilla sugar	1	pkg.
3	eggs	3	
30 mL	lemon juice	2	tbsp.
60 mL	water	4	tbsp.
200 g	all-purpose flour	1⅓	cups
4 g	**oetker** baking powder	1	tsp.
	pinch cinnamon		pinch
300 g	peeled, chopped apples	¾	lb.
50 g	chopped walnuts	½	cup
50 g	raisins	½	cup

Glaze:

250 g	sifted icing sugar	2	cups
30 mL	lemon juice	2	tbsp.
15-30 mL	hot water	1-2	tbsp.

Decoration:

Angelica, optional

Batter:
PREHEAT oven to 180°C (350°F). Grease a 24 cm (9½") spring form pan with centre insert. Sprinkle with bread crumbs.
CREAM butter, sugar and vanilla sugar together in mixer bowl.
BEAT in eggs, one at a time, lemon juice and water, beating until light and fluffy.
SIFT flour, baking powder and cinnamon together. Gradually beat into creamed mixture.
COMBINE apples, walnuts and raisins.
FOLD into batter.
TURN into prepared pan.
BAKE on lower oven rack at 180°C (350°F) for 60-70 minutes or until toothpick inserted in centre comes out clean.
COOL 10 minutes then remove from pan and cool slightly until just warm.
Glaze:
COMBINE icing sugar, lemon juice and water to make a thick glaze consistency. Pour over warm cake.
DECORATE with angelica if desired.

Cherry Crumb Cake

Batter:

150 g	butter	¾	cup
150 g	sugar	¾	cup
1 pkg	**oetker** vanilla sugar	1	pkg.
3	eggs	3	
6 drops	**oetker** lemon flavouring concentrate	6	drops
105 mL	water	7	tbsp.
200 g	all-purpose flour	1⅓	cups
4 g	**oetker** baking powder	1	tsp.

Filling:

500-750 g	fresh or canned cherries	1-1½	lbs.

Crumb Topping:

200 g	all-purpose flour	1⅓	cups
150 g	sugar	¾	cup
1 pkg	**oetker** vanilla sugar	1	pkg.
4 g	cinnamon	1	tsp.
150 g	unsalted (sweet) butter	¾	cup

Batter:
PREHEAT oven to 180°C (350°F). Grease a 2 L (39 cm × 26 cm/15" × 10") jelly roll pan.
CREAM butter, sugar and vanilla sugar together in mixer bowl.
BEAT in eggs, one at a time, lemon flavouring and water, beating until light and fluffy.
SIFT flour and baking powder together. Gradually beat into creamed mixture.
TURN batter into prepared pan.
Filling:
COVER with pitted, well drained cherries.
Crumb Topping:
COMBINE flour, sugar, vanilla sugar and cinnamon. CUT in butter, working it with fork to form crumbs. SPRINKLE evenly over cherries.
BAKE on middle oven rack at 180°C (350°F) for 45-55 minutes or until toothpick inserted in centre comes out clean.

Christmas Stollen (Fruit Cake)

Dough:

500 g	all-purpose flour	3⅓ cups
1 pkg	**oetker** baking powder (14 g/1 tbsp.)	1 pkg.
200 g	sifted icing sugar	1⅓ cups
1 pkg	**oetker** vanilla sugar	1 pkg.
2	eggs	2
1 btl	**oetker** rum flavouring concentrate	1 btl.
4 drops	**oetker** lemon flavouring concentrate	4 drops
4 drops	**oetker** almond flavouring concentrate	4 drops
250 g	quark, ricotta or creamed cottage cheese	1¼ cups
70 g	shortening	⅓ cup
120 g	butter	⅔ cup
120 g	raisins	1 cup
120 g	currants	1 cup
120 g	finely chopped almonds	1 cup
50 g	chopped, mixed candied peel	½ cup

Glaze:

50 g	melted butter	¼ cup
50 g	sifted icing sugar	⅓ cup

Dough:

PREHEAT oven to 230°C (450°F). Grease a 2 L (39 cm × 26 cm/15″ × 10″) jelly roll pan. Line with waxed paper. Grease again.

SIFT flour and baking powder together on pastry board. Make a well in centre.

PUT all ingredients except fruits in well.

KNEAD all ingredients together to make a smooth dough. Lastly knead raisins, currants, almonds and peel into dough.

SHAPE into a loaf on prepared pan. Flatten slightly.

BAKE on middle oven rack for 5 minutes at 230°C (450°F) then reduce oven to 180°C (350°F) and bake for 35-40 minutes or until golden.

BRUSH cake immediately after baking with melted butter. Cool.

SPRINKLE with icing sugar before serving.

Chocolate Orange Cake

Batter:

150 g	butter	¾ cup
150 g	sugar	¾ cup
1 pkg	**oetker** vanilla sugar	1 pkg.
6	egg yolks	6
150 g	all-purpose flour	1 cup
1 pkg	**oetker** baking powder (14 g/1 tbsp.)	1 pkg.
6 sq	semi-sweet chocolate, grated	6 sq.
100 g	ground almonds	1 cup
6	egg whites	6

Filling:

1 pkg	**oetker** vanilla pudding mix	1 pkg.
150 g	sugar	¾ cup
250 mL	milk	1 cup
250 mL	orange juice	1 cup
200 g	sweet (unsalted) butter	1 cup
4 sq	semi-sweet chocolate, melted	4 sq.

Decoration:

100 g	chocolate sprinkles orange slices	1 cup

Batter:
PREHEAT oven to 180°C (350°F). Grease and flour a 25 cm × 25 cm (10″ × 10″) cake pan.
CREAM butter, ⅔ of sugar, vanilla sugar and egg yolks together on high speed of electric mixer until light and creamy.
COMBINE flour, baking powder, grated chocolate and almonds. Mix well. Gradually add to creamed mixture.
BEAT egg whites and remaining ⅓ of sugar to stiff peaks.
FOLD egg whites into creamed mixture gently.
TURN batter into prepared pan.
BAKE on middle oven rack at 180°C (350°F) for 35-40 minutes.
REMOVE from pan immediately and cool completely.
SLICE cake horizontally with thread to make 2 layers.

Filling:
COMBINE vanilla pudding mix, sugar and 125 mL (½ cup) milk in small bowl. Stir until smoothly blended.
RINSE saucepan with cold water.
HEAT remaining milk to boiling. Stir in pudding mixture and orange juice. Bring to boil again, stirring constantly.
REMOVE from heat. Cool to room temperature, stirring occasionally.
CREAM butter. Beat in pudding 1 spoonful at a time. (Butter and pudding must be at same temperature to prevent curdling).
BLEND melted chocolate with ½ of pudding mixture and spread on bottom cake layer.
PLACE top cake layer over chocolate filling.
SPREAD remaining orange pudding mixture over top and sides of cake, reserving a little for decoration.
COVER sides with chocolate sprinkles.
DECORATE top attractively with reserved orange pudding mixture and orange slices.

Coffee Cream Pyramid

Coffee Cream Filling:

5	egg yolks	5
100 g	sugar	½ cup
1 pkg	**oetker** vanilla sugar	1 pkg.
75 mL	strong, black coffee	5 tbsp.
1 btl	**oetker** rum flavouring concentrate	1 btl.
250 g	sweet (unsalted) butter	1¼ cups
42	lady fingers	42
125 mL	cherry brandy	½ cup

Decoration:

4 sq	chocolate, shaved candied cherries	4 sq.

Filling:
COMBINE egg yolks, sugar, vanilla sugar, coffee and rum flavouring in top of double boiler. Beat over simmering water until thick and creamy.
REMOVE from heat. Continue beating till cool.
CREAM butter. Add to coffee mixture, one spoonful at a time, beating until light and creamy.
SPRINKLE lady fingers with cherry brandy.
ARRANGE layer of lady fingers on cake plate to form bottom of pyramid (4 across and 3 lengthwise).
SPREAD evenly with some of filling.
COVER with another row of 4 × 3 lady fingers.
SPREAD evenly with filling.
SHAPE cake into pyramid by continuing alternate layers of 3 across × 3 down lady fingers, filling, 2 × 3 lady fingers, filling, 1 × 3 lady fingers (forming top of pyramid).
SPREAD sides of pyramid with remaining filling.
SPRINKLE with shaved chocolate. Decorate top with cherries. Chill until serving.

Rose Cake

Dough:

200 g	quark, ricotta or creamed cottage cheese	1	cup
100 mL	milk	½	cup
1	egg	1	
125 mL	oil	½	cup
100 g	sugar	½	cup
1 pkg	**oetker** vanilla sugar	1	pkg.
pinch	salt		pinch
400 g	all-purpose flour	2⅔	cups
1 pkg	**oetker** baking powder (14 g/1 tbsp.)	1	pkg.
50 g	melted butter	¼	cup

Filling:

150 g	ground almonds	1½	cups
150 g	chopped raisins	1¼	cups
50 g	chopped mixed candied peel	¼	cup
50 g	icing sugar	½	cup
1 pkg	**oetker** vanilla sugar	1	pkg.
4 g	cinnamon	1	tsp.
50 mL	red currant jam or marmalade	¼	cup
15 mL	rum	1	tbsp.

Dough:
PREHEAT oven to 180°C (350°F). Grease and flour a 26 cm (10½") spring form pan with centre insert.
COMBINE cheese, milk, egg, oil, sugar, vanilla sugar and salt. Stir until smoothly blended.
SIFT flour and baking powder together. Beat ⅔ of flour mixture into creamed mixture.
KNEAD remaining flour into dough.
ROLL out dough on floured board to a 50 cm × 40 cm (20" × 16") rectangle.
BRUSH with half of melted butter.
Filling:
COMBINE almonds, raisins, peel, icing sugar, vanilla sugar, cinnamon, jam and rum. Stir until well blended.
DISTRIBUTE filling evenly over dough.
ROLL up dough starting with longer side.
CUT into 2 cm (¾") thick slices.
PLACE slices upright in baking pan, starting with outer rim and then place around inner rim of pan.
BRUSH with remaining melted butter.
BAKE on middle oven rack at 180°C (350°F) for 40-50 minutes or until golden brown.
REMOVE from pan immediately and let cool. Sprinkle with icing sugar before serving.

Easter Crescent

Filling:

150 g	shredded coconut	1¾	cups
250 g	apricot jam	¾	cup
50 mL	rum	¼	cup

Dough:

150 g	quark, ricotta or creamed cottage cheese	⅔	cup
125 mL	milk	½	cup
125 mL	oil	½	cup
80 g	sugar	⅓	cup
1 pkg	**oetker** vanilla sugar	1	pkg.
pinch	salt		pinch
325 g	all-purpose flour	2¼	cups
1 pkg	**oetker** baking powder (14 g/1 tbsp.)	1	pkg.

Filling:
COMBINE all the filling ingredients in a bowl; set aside.
Dough:
PREHEAT oven to 180°C (350°F).
GREASE a baking sheet.
COMBINE cheese, milk, oil, sugar, vanilla sugar and salt, until smoothly blended.
SIFT flour and baking powder together. Stir ⅔ of the flour into the cheese mixture. Gently knead the remaining flour into the dough.
ROLL out dough on a well floured board to a 35 cm (14") square.
ROLL up dough, starting from a corner.
SHAPE roll into a crescent on the baking sheet.
BAKE on middle oven rack at 180°C (350°F) for 35-40 minutes or until golden.
COOL completely.
SPRINKLE with icing sugar before serving.

Sour Cream Nut Ring

Batter:

200 g	butter	¾ cup
225 g	sugar	1 cup
1 pkg	**oetker** vanilla sugar	1 pkg.
2	eggs	2
½ btl	**oetker** lemon flavouring concentrate	½ btl.
3 drops	**oetker** almond flavouring concentrate	3 drops
225 g	all-purpose flour	1⅔ cups
1 pkg	**oetker** baking powder (14 g/1 tbsp.)	1 pkg.
250 mL	sour cream	1 cup

Filling:

75 g	brown sugar	½ cup
100 g	ground hazelnuts	1 cup
5 mL	cinnamon	1 tsp.

Glaze:

50 mL	hot apricot jam	¼ cup
1	egg white	1
125 g	sifted icing sugar	1 cup

Batter:
PREHEAT oven to 180°C (350°F).
GREASE and flour a 24 cm (9½") spring form pan with a fluted centre tube insert.
CREAM butter, sugar, vanilla sugar, eggs and flavouring concentrates together until light and fluffy.
SIFT flour and baking powder together. Add to butter mixture, alternately with the sour cream, beating until well blended.

Filling:
COMBINE brown sugar, hazelnuts and cinnamon.
SPREAD ⅓ of batter into prepared pan. Spread ½ of filling over batter.
CAREFULLY spread ½ remaining batter over the filling, then cover with all the remaining filling.
COVER with remaining batter.
BAKE on middle oven rack at 180°C (350°F) for 55-60 minutes or until toothpick inserted in centre comes out clean.
COOL in pan 10 minutes then remove cake from pan.
SPREAD hot apricot jam over cake to cover top and sides. Cool cake completely.

Glaze:
BLEND egg white and icing sugar until smooth.
Drizzle over cake.

Mother's Day Heart

Batter:

150	g	butter	¾	cup
150	g	sugar	¾	cup
1	pkg	**oetker** vanilla sugar	1	pkg.
4		eggs	4	
1	btl	**oetker** rum flavouring concentrate	1	btl.
6	sq	semi-sweet chocolate, melted	6	sq.
150	g	all-purpose flour	1	cup
8	g	**oetker** baking powder	2	tsp.
100	g	shredded coconut	⅔	cup

Filling and Decoration:

50	mL	hot red currant jam or marmalade	¼	cup
125	mL	whipping cream	½	cup
½	pkg	**oetker** Whip it	½	pkg.
15	g	icing sugar	2	tbsp.
1	pkg	**oetker** vanilla sugar	1	pkg.

Batter:
PREHEAT oven to 180°C (350°F). Grease and flour heart shaped spring form pan.
CREAM butter, sugar, vanilla sugar, eggs, rum flavouring and melted chocolate together in mixer bowl. Beat at medium speed until light and fluffy.
SIFT flour and baking powder together. Fold in gentl but thoroughly.
FOLD in coconut.
TURN batter into prepared pan.
BAKE on lower oven rack at 180°C (350°F) for 40-4 minutes or until toothpick inserted in centre comes ou clean.
REMOVE from pan immediately and let cool completely.
SPREAD hot jam or marmalade over top and sides o cake.

Decoration:
BEAT cream to soft peaks. Gradually add Whip it, icing sugar and vanilla sugar, beating to stiff peaks.
DECORATE cake attractively with whipped cream.

Walnut Boats

Pastry:

170 g	all-purpose flour	1¼ cups
pinch	**oetker** baking powder	pinch
30 g	ground almonds	⅓ cup
100 g	sifted icing sugar	⅔ cup
1 pkg	**oetker** vanilla sugar	1 pkg.
1 btl	**oetker** lemon flavouring concentrate	1 btl.
1	egg yolk	1
120 g	butter	⅔ cup

Filling:

100 g	ground walnuts	1 cup
50 g	sugar	¼ cup
1 pkg	**oetker** vanilla sugar	1 pkg.
pinch	cinnamon	pinch
pinch	cloves	pinch
2 sq	semi-sweet chocolate, grated	2 sq.
15 mL	red currant jam or marmalade	1 tbsp.
1	egg white	1

Decoration:

	candied cherries, halved

Pastry:
PREHEAT oven to 200°C (400°F). Grease and flour small oval shaped baking forms.
SIFT flour and baking powder together onto pastry board.
SPRINKLE with ground almonds. Make well in centre.
PUT icing sugar, vanilla sugar, flavouring and egg yolk in well. Work a little of flour into centre mixture.
CUT butter into small pieces over flour mixture.
WORK all ingredients together quickly to make a smooth dough.
CHILL slightly for easy rolling (about ½ hour).
RESERVE ¼ of dough.
ROLL out remaining dough on a lightly floured surface to 5 mm (¼") thickness.
CUT and fit into baking forms.
Filling:
COMBINE ground walnuts, sugar, vanilla sugar, cinnamon, cloves, grated chocolate, jam and egg white. Mix well.
FILL pastry with nut mixture.
ROLL out remaining pastry.
CUT into 2 cm (¾") rounds and place over filling.
COVER with cherry half.
BAKE on middle oven rack at 200°C (400°F) for 15-20 minutes or until pastry is golden.

Almond Speculaas

Dough:

500 g	all-purpose flour	3⅓ cups
1 pkg	**oetker** baking powder (14g/1 tbsp.)	1 pkg.
250 g	sifted icing sugar	1⅔ cups
1 pkg	**oetker** vanilla sugar	1 pkg.
2	eggs	2
1	egg yolk	1
1 btl	**oetker** lemon flavouring concentrate	1 btl
3 drops	**oetker** almond flavouring concentrate	3 drops
4 g	cinnamon	1 tsp.
250 g	sweet (unsalted) butter	1¼ cups
1	egg white, slightly beaten	1

Decoration:

100 g	sliced almonds	1 cup

Dough:
PREHEAT oven to 200°C (400°F). Grease a baking sheet.
COMBINE flour and baking powder together on pastry board. Make a well in centre.
PUT icing sugar, vanilla sugar, eggs, egg yolk, flavourings and cinnamon in well.
WORK a little of flour into centre mixture.
CUT butter into small pieces over flour mixture.
WORK all ingredients together quickly to make a smooth dough.
CHILL slightly for easy rolling (about ½ hour).
ROLL out dough on lightly floured surface to 5 mm (¼") thickness.
CUT dough into 5 cm × 3 cm (2" × 1¼") rectangles.
BRUSH with egg white.
SPRINKLE with almonds.
PLACE on prepared baking sheet.
BAKE on middle oven rack at 200°C (400°F) for 8-12 minutes or until light golden.

Pinwheel Refrigerator Cookies

Dough:

250 g	all-purpose flour	1⅔ cups	
4 g	**oetker** baking powder	1 tsp.	
150 g	sugar	¾ cup	
1 pkg	**oetker** vanilla sugar	1 pkg.	
1 btl	**oetker** rum flavouring concentrate	1 btl.	
1	egg	1	
120 g	sweet (unsalted) butter	1¼ cups	
20 g	cocoa	2 tbsp.	
20 g	sugar	2 tbsp.	
15 mL	milk	1 tbsp.	
1	egg white	1	

Dough:
SIFT flour and baking powder onto pastry board. Make a well in centre.
PUT sugar, vanilla sugar, flavouring and egg in well.
WORK a little flour into centre mixture.
CUT butter into small pieces. Quickly work all ingredients together into a smooth dough.
CHILL slightly for easy rolling (about ½ hour).
DIVIDE dough into 2 equal portions.
COMBINE cocoa, sugar and milk. Stir well.
KNEAD into one portion of dough.
ROLL out white and dark dough into rectangles of equal size about 3 mm (⅛″) thick.
BRUSH white dough with egg white.
PLACE dark dough on top of white dough.
ROLL up tightly jelly-roll fashion into rolls of 3 cm (1¼″) diameter. Chill until firm.
PREHEAT oven to 180°C (350°F).
CUT roll with sharp knife into 6 mm (¼″) slices.
PLACE on greased baking sheet.
BAKE on middle oven rack at 180°C (350°F) for 10-12 minutes or until light golden.

Sand Tartlets

Dough:

250 g	all-purpose flour	1⅔ cups	
80 g	sifted icing sugar	⅔ cup	
1 pkg	**oetker** vanilla sugar	1 pkg.	
½ btl	**oetker** lemon flavouring concentrate	½ btl.	
50 g	almond paste	2 oz.	
200 g	sweet (unsalted) butter, cut into small pieces	1 cup	
1	egg yolk, beaten	1	
100 g	coarse granulated sugar crystals	½ cup	

Dough:
PREHEAT oven to 180°C (350°F). Grease baking sheet.
SIFT flour onto pastry board.
COMBINE with icing sugar, vanilla sugar, lemon flavouring, almond paste and butter.
WORK all ingredients together to make a smooth dough.
SHAPE into a roll 4 cm (1½″) in diameter.
CHILL until firm.
BRUSH egg yolk onto roll.
SPRINKLE with coarse granulated sugar.
CUT into slices 6 mm (¼″) thick.
PLACE on baking sheet and bake on middle oven rack at 180°C (350°F) for 10-15 minutes or until golden.

Hermits

Dough:

180 g	butter	⅞ cup	
200 g	sugar	1 cup	
1 pkg	**oetker** vanilla sugar	1 pkg.	
1 btl	**oetker** rum flavouring concentrate	1 btl.	
2	eggs	2	
350 g	all-purpose flour	2⅓ cups	
1 pkg	**oetker** baking powder (14 g/1 tbsp)	1 pkg.	
4 g	cinnamon	1 tsp.	
125 mL	cold, strong coffee	½ cup	
150 g	chopped walnuts or hazelnuts	1 cup	
100 g	raisins	1 cup	

Decoration:

jam, hazelnuts or walnuts

Dough:
PREHEAT oven to 180°C (350°F). Grease a baking sheet.
CREAM butter, sugar, vanilla sugar and rum flavouring together until light and fluffy.
STIR in eggs.
SIFT flour, baking powder and cinnamon together.
ADD flour and coffee alternately to creamed mixture.
STIR in nuts and raisins.
PLACE small paper baking cups on baking sheet.
SPOON dough into paper baking cups.
BAKE on middle oven rack at 180°C (350°F) for 20-30 minutes or until golden.
DECORATE with a jam and nuts.

Chocolate Kisses with Whipping Cream

Batter:

5	egg yolks	5
150 g	sugar	¾ cup
1 pkg	**oetker** vanilla sugar	1 pkg.
½ btl	**oetker** rum flavouring concentrate	½ btl.
5	egg whites	5
110 g	all-purpose flour	¾ cup
1 g	**oetker** baking powder	¼ tsp.

Filling:

250 mL	whipping cream	1 cup
1 pkg	**oetker** Whip it	1 pkg.
2 pkg	**oetker** vanilla sugar	2 pkg.
125 mL	strained apricot jam	½ cup

Glaze:

1 pkg	**oetker** Chocofix OR	1 pkg.
7 sq	semi-sweet chocolate	7 sq.
100 g	sweet (unsalted) butter	½ cup
½ btl	**oetker** rum flavouring concentrate	½ btl.

Batter:
PREHEAT oven to 180°C (350°F). Grease and flour 18 large muffin cups.
COMBINE egg yolks, sugar, vanilla sugar and rum flavouring in mixer bowl. Beat at high speed of electric mixer until thick and creamy.
BEAT egg whites to stiff peaks.
SIFT flour and baking powder over egg yolk mixture and fold in gently but thoroughly.
FOLD in egg whites gently.
TURN batter into muffin pans.
BAKE on middle oven rack at 180°C (350°F) for 18-23 minutes.
REMOVE from baking pan immediately. Let cool completely.
SLICE in half horizontally with thread.
Filling:
BEAT whipping cream to soft peaks. Gradually add Whip it and vanilla sugar, beating to stiff peaks.
Glaze:
PLACE pouch of Chocofix in boiling water to soften contents. OR combine chocolate, butter and rum flavouring in top of double boiler, stirring constantly until smoothly melted.
SPREAD bottom half of cakes with jam. Spread filling over jam and cover with top cake layers.
SPREAD glaze evenly over top and sides of cakes. Let set. Makes 18 chocolate kisses.

Cream filled Puff Pastries

Pastry:

2 pkg	frozen puff pastry OR	2 pkg.
200 g	softened butter	1 cup
480 g	all-purpose flour	3¼ cups
175 mL	ice water	¾ cup
200 g	cold butter	1 cup
1	egg	1

Filling:

250 mL	whipping cream	1 cup
1 pkg	**oetker** Whip it	1 pkg.
1 pkg	**oetker** vanilla sugar	1 pkg.

Glaze:

1 pkg	**oetker** Chocofix OR	1 pkg.
7 sq	semi-sweet chocolate	7 sq.
100 g	sweet (unsalted) butter	½ cup

Pastry:
PREHEAT oven to 200°C (400°F). Grease funnel forms.
THAW puff pastry according to package directions OR refer to Vol. I, Page 17 for "Puff Pastry"
ROLL out pastry to rectangle 40 × 35 cm (16" × 14").
CUT pastry to 5 cm × 35 cm (2" × 14") strips.
WRAP around funnel forms.
BEAT egg slightly.
BRUSH pastry with egg.
PLACE funnel forms onto moist baking sheet.
BAKE at 200°C (400°F) on middle oven rack for 10-15 minutes or until golden.
REMOVE pastry immediately from funnel forms and let cool completely.
Filling:
BEAT whipping cream to soft peaks. Gradually add Whip it and vanilla sugar, beating to stiff peaks.
Glaze:
PLACE pouch of Chocofix in boiling water to soften contents, OR combine chocolate and butter in top of double boiler.
PLACE over boiling water, stirring constantly until smoothly melted.
FILL pastry with whipping cream. Drizzle with chocolate. Chill until serving.

Strawberry Tarts

Pastry:

180 g	all-purpose flour	1¼ cups
4 g	**oetker** baking powder	1 tsp.
70 g	icing sugar, sifted	½ cup
1 pkg	**oetker** vanilla sugar	1 pkg.
1	egg	1
70 g	butter or margarine, cold	⅓ cup

Filling:

250 mL	whipping cream	1 cup
1 pkg	**oetker** Whip it	1 pkg.
1 pkg	**oetker** vanilla sugar	1 pkg.
50 g	sugar	⅓ cup

Decoration:

300 g	fresh strawberries	2 cups

Pastry:
PREHEAT oven to 200°C (400°F). Grease 12-15 fluted tart pans.
SIFT flour and baking powder onto pastry board. Make a well in centre.
PUT icing sugar, vanilla sugar and egg in well. Work a little flour into centre mixture.
CUT cold butter into small pieces over flour mixture.
WORK all ingredients together quickly to make a smooth dough. Chill slightly for easy rolling (about ½ hour).
ROLL out dough on floured surface to 5 mm (¼") thickness.
CUT out rounds with a floured cutter 9 cm (3½") diameter.
FIT into prepared tart pans.
GREASE 12-15 empty tart forms on the outside and fit inside pastry of filled pans.
BAKE on middle oven rack at 200°C (400°F) for 10-15 minutes or until golden.
REMOVE from forms immediately and let cool completely.

Filling:
BEAT whipping cream to soft peaks. Gradually add Whip it, vanilla sugar and sugar, beating to stiff peaks.
DECORATE tarts with whipped cream and strawberries.

Chocolate Glazed Nut Kisses

Dough:

2	eggs	2
200 g	sugar	1 cup
1 pkg	**oetker** vanilla sugar	1 pkg.
pinch	**oetker** baking powder	pinch
pinch	salt	pinch
pinch	ground cloves	pinch
pinch	cinnamon	pinch
6 drops	**oetker** lemon flavouring concentrate	6 drops
70 g	chopped candied orange peel	¾ cup
120 g	ground almonds	1¼ cups
100 g	ground hazelnuts	1 cup
	round wafers	

Decoration:

½ pkg	**oetker** Chocofix	½ pkg.
	OR	
4 sq	semi-sweet chocolate	4 sq.
50 g	sweet (unsalted) butter	¼ cup

Dough:
PREHEAT oven to 180°C (350°F).
BEAT eggs, sugar and vanilla sugar at high speed of electric mixer until thick and creamy.
FOLD baking powder, salt, cloves, cinnamon, lemon flavouring, orange peel, almonds and hazelnuts into creamed mixture.
DROP by teaspoon onto thin round wafers (approx. 5 cm/2" diameter).
PLACE on baking sheet.
BAKE on middle oven rack at 180°C (350°F) for 30-35 minutes or until golden.
LET cool.

Decoration:
PLACE pouch of Chocofix into boiling water to soften contents OR
COMBINE chocolate and butter in top of double boiler.
PLACE over boiling water, stirring constantly until smoothly melted.
DRIZZLE chocolate glaze over cookies.

Lemon Snow Dreams

Batter:

5	egg yolks	5
150 g	sugar	¾ cup
1 pkg	**oetker** vanilla sugar	1 pkg.
5	egg whites	5
110 g	all-purpose flour	¾ cup
1 g	**oetker** baking powder	¼ tsp.

Lemon Cream Filling:

1 pkg	**oetker** vanilla pudding mix	1 pkg.
150 g	sugar	¾ cup
500 mL	milk	2 cups
45 mL	lemon juice	3 tbsp.
200 g	sweet (unsalted) butter	1 cup

Decoration:

100 g	shredded coconut lemon slices	1 cup

Batter:
PREHEAT oven to 180°C (350°F). Grease a 2 L (39 cm × 26 cm/15″ × 10″) jelly roll pan and line with waxed paper. Grease again.
COMBINE egg yolks, sugar and vanilla sugar in mixer bowl. Beat at high speed of electric mixer until thick and creamy.
BEAT egg whites to stiff peaks.
SIFT flour and baking powder together over egg yolk mixture and fold in gently.
FOLD in egg whites gently.
SPREAD batter evenly in jelly roll pan.
BAKE on middle oven rack at 180°C (350°F) for 10-12 minutes.
TURN out immediately. Remove waxed paper from cake bottom. Cool.
CUT into 6 cm (2½″) rounds.

Filling:
COMBINE vanilla pudding mix, sugar and 125 mL (½ cup) milk in small bowl. Stir until smoothly blended.
RINSE saucepan with cold water.
HEAT remaining 375 mL (1½ cups) milk to boiling. Stir in pudding mixture. Bring to a boil, stirring constantly.
REMOVE from heat.
ADD lemon juice.
COOL to room temperature, stirring occasionally.
CREAM butter. Beat in pudding 1 spoonful at a time. (Butter and pudding must be at same temperature to prevent curdling.)
FILL half the baked cake rounds with cream filling.
PLACE remaining rounds over filling.
SPREAD filling on top and sides of rounds, reserving a little for decoration.
SPRINKLE with coconut and decorate with cream filling and lemon slices.

Dominoes

Batter:

200 g	butter	1 cup
200 g	sifted icing sugar	1½ cups
1 pkg	**oetker** vanilla sugar	1 pkg.
5 drops	**oetker** lemon flavouring concentrate	5 drops
5	eggs	5
100 g	all-purpose flour	⅔ cup
8 g	**oetker** baking powder	2 tsp.
2 mL	cinnamon	½ tsp.
2 mL	ground cloves	½ tsp.
200 g	ground almonds	2 cups
8 sq	semi-sweet chocolate, grated	8 sq.

Batter:
PREHEAT oven to 180°C (350°F). Grease a 2 L (39 cm × 26 cm/15″ × 10″) jelly roll pan and line with waxed paper. Grease again.
CREAM butter, icing sugar, vanilla sugar and lemon flavouring together until light and fluffy.
BEAT in eggs one at a time.
SIFT flour, baking powder, cinnamon and cloves together over creamed mixture. Mix well.
STIR in almonds and chocolate.
SPREAD batter evenly in prepared pan.
BAKE on middle oven rack at 180°C (350°F) for 20-25 minutes.
REMOVE waxed paper immediately after baking and let cake cool completely.

Continued on page 68.

Dominoes (cont.)

Chocolate glaze:

1 pkg	**oetker** Chocofix	1 pkg.	
	OR		
7 sq	semi-sweet chocolate	7 sq.	
100 g	sweet (unsalted) butter	½ cup	

Egg White Glaze:

1	egg white	1	
150 g	sifted icing sugar	1¼ cups	

Chocolate Glaze:
SOFTEN Chocofix as directed on package
OR
COMBINE chocolate and butter in top of double boiler. Place over boiling water, stirring constantly until smoothly melted.
SPREAD over cake. Let cool until set.
CUT into rectangles (4 cm × 6 cm/1½″ × 2¼″).
COMBINE egg white and sifted icing sugar, stirring until smooth.
DECORATE domino squares with white icing.

Layered Stars

Dough:

300 g	all-purpose flour	2 cups	
8 g	**oetker** baking powder	2 tsp.	
100 g	sifted icing sugar	1 cup	
1 pkg	**oetker** vanilla sugar	1 pkg.	
1	egg	1	
150 g	butter, cold	¾ cup	

Filling:

	red currant jelly
	icing sugar

Dough:
PREHEAT oven to 180°C (350°F). Grease a baking sheet.
COMBINE flour and baking powder together on pastry board. Make a well in centre.
PUT icing sugar, vanilla sugar and egg in well. Work little of dry ingredients into centre of mixture.
CUT cold butter in small pieces over flour mixture.
WORK all ingredients together quickly to make a smooth dough. Chill slightly for easy rolling (about ½ hour).
ROLL out dough on floured surface to 6 mm (¼″) thickness.
CUT into star shapes, equal amounts of 3 different sizes.
PLACE on prepared baking sheet.
BAKE on middle oven rack at 180°C (350°F) for 8-10 minutes or until light golden.
SPREAD jam on bottom of middle size stars and place on top of large stars.
SPREAD jam on bottom of small stars and place on top of middle stars.
SPRINKLE with sifted icing sugar.

Almond Buttons

Batter:

250 g	all-purpose flour	1⅔ cups	
4 g	**oetker** baking powder	1 tsp.	
100 g	sugar	½ cup	
1 pkg	**oetker** vanilla sugar	1 pkg.	
pinch	salt	pinch	
3	egg yolks	3	
150 g	butter	¾ cup	

Decoration:

1	egg white, slightly beaten	1	
50 g	chopped almonds	½ cup	
	red jam or jelly		

Batter:
PREHEAT oven to 180°C (350°F). Grease a baking sheet.
COMBINE flour and baking powder together on pastry board. Make a well in centre.
PUT sugar, vanilla sugar, salt and egg yolks in centre Work a little of dry ingredients into centre mixture.
CUT cold butter in small pieces over flour mixture.
WORK all ingredients together quickly to make a smooth dough. Chill slightly for easy shaping (about ½ hour).
SHAPE dough into 2.5 cm (1″) balls.
PLACE on prepared baking sheet.
BRUSH each ball with beaten egg white.
SPRINKLE with almonds.
PRESS indentation in middle of each ball.
FILL with jam.
BAKE on middle oven rack at 180°C (350°F) for 10-15 minutes or until golden.

Pistachio Yummies

Dough:

200 g	all-purpose flour	1⅓	cups
4 g	**oetker** baking powder	1	tsp.
100 g	sifted icing sugar	¾	cup
1 pkg	**oetker** vanilla sugar	1	pkg.
100 g	ground almonds	1	cup
175 g	butter	¾	cup

Filling:

50 mL	apricot jam or marmalade	¼	cup

Glaze:

1 pkg	**oetker** Chocofix OR	1	pkg.
7 sq	semi-sweet chocolate	7	sq.
100 g	sweet (unsalted) butter	½	cup

Decoration:

30 g	finely chopped pistachio nuts	¼	cup

Dough:
PREHEAT oven to 200°C (400°F). Grease a baking sheet.
COMBINE flour and baking powder together on pastry board. Make a well in centre.
PUT icing sugar, vanilla sugar and almonds in well.
CUT cold butter in small pieces over flour.
WORK all ingredients together quickly to make a smooth dough. Chill slightly for easy rolling (about ½ hour).
ROLL out dough on floured surface to 6 mm (¼") thickness.
CUT into 5 cm (2") diameter rounds.
PLACE on prepared baking sheet.
BAKE on middle oven rack at 200°C (400°F) for 8-12 minutes or until golden.
LET cool completely.
SPREAD jam on half of cookies. Cover with remaining cookies.
Glaze:
SOFTEN Chocofix as directed on package OR
COMBINE chocolate and butter in top of double boiler. Place over boiling water, stirring constantly until smoothly melted.
SPREAD over top of cookies.
DECORATE with chopped pistachios.

Fried Triangle Cookies

Batter:

250 g	all-purpose flour	1⅔	cups
4 g	**oetker** baking powder	1	tsp.
4	egg yolks	4	
3 pkg	**oetker** vanilla sugar	3	pkg.
pinch	salt		pinch
15 mL	rum	1	tbsp.
75 mL	sour cream	⅓	cup

Decoration:

50 g	sifted icing sugar	½	cup
1 pkg	**oetker** vanilla sugar	1	pkg.

For deep frying:

oil or shortening

Batter:
COMBINE flour and baking powder together on pastry board. Make a well in centre.
PUT egg yolks, vanilla sugar, salt, rum and sour cream in well.
WORK all ingredients together quickly to make a smooth dough.
ROLL out dough to 6 mm (¼") thickness.
FOLD sides of dough into centre. Chill for about 10 minutes.
REPEAT rolling, folding, and chilling 2 more times.
ROLL out dough to 6 mm (¼") thickness.
CUT out small triangles.
HEAT oil or shortening to 190°C (375°F). Fry triangles, a few at a time, until golden brown.
REMOVE from fat. Drain on paper towelling.
COMBINE icing sugar and vanilla sugar.
SPRINKLE over triangles.

Cocoa Meringues

Meringue:

3	egg whites	3
150 g	sugar	¾ cup
15 g	sifted cocoa	2 tbsp.

Filling:

250 mL	whipping cream	1 cup
1 pkg	**oetker** Whip it	1 pkg.
1 pkg	**oetker** vanilla sugar	1 pkg.
1 btl	**oetker** rum flavouring concentrate	1 btl.

Decoration:

red currant jelly

Meringue:
PREHEAT oven to 70°C (150°F). Grease a baking sheet. Line with waxed paper. Grease again.
BEAT egg whites to soft peaks. Gradually add sugar and sifted, cocoa, beating to stiff peaks.
PUT meringue into decorator bag with large star tube
SPREAD spirals 8 cm/3″ long onto baking sheet.
BAKE on middle oven rack at 70°C (150°F) for 70-9 minutes or until dry.
COOL completely.
Filling:
BEAT whipping cream to soft peaks. Gradually add Whip it, vanilla sugar and rum flavouring, beating to stiff peaks.
PUT into decorator bag with tube.
PRESS whipped cream onto under side of half the baked meringues.
PLACE remaining meringues on top with underside (filling.
PLACE meringues on edge and press remaining whipped cream on top edge.
DECORATE attractively with red currant jelly.

Mocha Meringue Surprises

Meringue:

4	egg whites	4
pinch	cream of tartar	pinch
200 g	sugar	1 cup
1 pkg	**oetker** vanilla sugar	1 pkg.
3 drops	**oetker** almond flavouring concentrate	3 drops
½ btl	**oetker** rum flavouring concentrate	½ btl.
100 g	ground almonds	1 cup

Filling:

250 mL	whipping cream	1 cup
1 pkg	**oetker** Whip it	1 pkg.
15 mL	brandy	1 tbsp.
½ btl	**oetker** rum flavouring concentrate	½ btl.
1 pkg	**oetker** vanilla sugar	1 pkg.
8 g	instant coffee powder	2 tsp.

Decoration:

grated chocolate
maraschino cherries

Meringue:
PREHEAT oven to 70°C (150°F). Grease a baking sheet. Line with waxed paper. Grease again.
BEAT egg whites and cream of tartar to soft peaks. Gradually add sugar, vanilla sugar and flavourings, beating to stiff peaks.
FOLD in almonds gently.
PUT mixture into decorating bag with large round tube.
SPREAD rounds 7 cm (2¾″) in diameter onto baking sheet.
BAKE on middle oven rack at 70°C (150°F) for 70-9 minutes or until dry.
COOL completely.
Filling:
BEAT whipping cream to soft peaks. Gradually add Whip it, brandy, rum flavouring, vanilla sugar and coffee, beating to stiff peaks.
PUT filling into decorating bag with star tube.
SPREAD ¾ of filling on half the baked meringue rounds.
SPRINKLE with grated chocolate.
COVER with remaining meringue rounds.
DECORATE attractively with remaining filling, a litt grated chocolate and maraschino cherries.

Glazed Marzipan Rounds

Dough:

350 g	all-purpose flour	2⅓	cups
4 g	**oetker** baking powder	1	tsp.
50 g	ground almonds	½	cup
200 g	sifted icing sugar	1½	cups
1 pkg	**oetker** vanilla sugar	1	pkg.
2	eggs	2	
1 btl	**oetker** lemon flavouring concentrate	1	btl.
175 g	sweet (unsalted) butter	¾	cup

Filling:

250 g	almond paste	8	oz.
30 g	apricot jam or marmalade	3	tbsp.
50 g	icing sugar	½	cup
15 mL	lemon juice	1	tbsp.

Frosting:

200 g	sifted icing sugar	1½	cups
15 mL	orange juice	1	tbsp.
15-30 mL	hot water	1-2	tbsp.

Decoration:

	candied cherries

Dough:
PREHEAT oven to 220°C (425°F). Grease 2 baking sheets.
COMBINE flour, baking powder and ground almond on pastry board. Make a well in centre.
PUT icing sugar, vanilla sugar, eggs and flavouring in well.
WORK dry ingredients into egg mixture.
CUT cold butter into small pieces. Quickly work into flour mixture to form a smooth dough.
CHILL slightly for easy rolling (about ½ hour).
ROLL out dough on floured surface to 6 mm (¼") thickness.
CUT into 5 cm (2") rounds with floured cutter.
PLACE on prepared baking sheets.
BAKE on middle oven rack at 220°C (425°F) for 12-15 minutes or until golden.
Filling:
KNEAD all ingredients together into a smooth paste.
ROLL out to 6 mm (¼") thickness.
CUT into 5 cm (2" diameter) rounds.
PLACE almond paste rounds between two cookies.
Glaze:
COMBINE all glaze ingredients adding enough water to make a smooth glaze consistency.
SPREAD glaze over top of cookies.
DECORATE with cherries.

Ginger Stars

Dough:

500 g	all-purpose flour	3⅓	cups
8 g	**oetker** baking powder	2	tsp.
80 g	ground walnuts	¾	cup
70 g	ground hazelnuts	⅔	cup
200 g	sifted icing sugar	1⅓	cup
1 pkg	**oetker** vanilla sugar	1	pkg.
8 g	ground ginger	2	tsp.
2	eggs	2	
½ btl	**oetker** lemon flavouring concentrate	½	btl.
250 g	butter	1¼	cups

Glaze:

250 g	sifted icing sugar	1⅔	cups
½ btl	**oetker** lemon flavouring concentrate	½	btl.
30-60 mL	hot water	2-4	tbsp.

Decoration:

100 g	coloured sugar sprinkles	1	cup

Dough:
PREHEAT oven to 200°C (400°F). Grease a baking sheet.
COMBINE flour, baking powder and ground nuts on pastry board. Make a well in centre.
PUT icing sugar, vanilla sugar, ginger, eggs and flavouring in well.
WORK dry ingredients into egg mixture.
CUT cold butter into small pieces. Quickly work into flour mixture to form a smooth dough.
CHILL slightly for easy rolling (about ½ hour).
ROLL out dough on floured surface to 6 mm (¼") thickness.
CUT out stars.
PLACE on prepared baking sheet.
BAKE on middle oven rack at 200°C (400°F) for 10-15 minutes or until golden.
LET cool completely.
Glaze:
COMBINE sifted icing sugar, flavouring and enough hot water to make a smooth glaze consistency.
SPREAD over top of cookies.
DECORATE with sprinkles.

Nut Swirls

Dough:

500	g	all-purpose flour	3⅓ cups
1	pkg	**oetker** instant dry yeast	1 pkg.
	pinch	salt	pinch
60	g	sugar	⅓ cup
1	pkg	**oetker** vanilla sugar	1 pkg.
3		egg yolks	3
½	btl	**oetker** lemon flavouring concentrate	½ btl.
125	g	melted butter	½ cup
250	mL	lukewarm milk	1 cup

Filling:

125	mL	milk	½ cup
50	g	butter	¼ cup
250	g	sugar	1¼ cups
1	pkg	**oetker** vanilla sugar	1 pkg.
½	btl	**oetker** lemon flavouring concentrate	½ btl.
1	btl	**oetker** rum flavouring concentrate	1 btl.
4	g	cinnamon	1 tsp.
300	g	ground walnuts	3 cups
50	g	dry bread crumbs	½ cup

Dough:
PREHEAT oven to 180°C (350°F). Grease a 28 cm (11″) spring form pan.
COMBINE ⅔ of flour, yeast and salt in large mixing bowl. Make a well in centre.
PUT sugar, vanilla sugar, egg yolks, flavouring and melted butter in well.
MIX ingredients, working from centre, gradually adding milk.
BEAT dough until it has a shiny, blistered appearance.
KNEAD remaining ⅓ of flour into dough until smooth, elastic and no longer sticky.
LET rise, covered, in warm place for 30 minutes.
ROLL out dough on lightly floured surface to a rectangle 25 cm × 60 cm (10″ × 24″).

Filling:
COMBINE milk, butter, sugar and vanilla sugar in saucepan. Bring to a boil. Remove from heat.
ADD flavourings, cinnamon, nuts and bread crumbs. Mix well. Cool completely.
COVER dough with filling.
ROLL up, starting at longer side. Place into prepared spring form pan. Brush with milk.
SET aside to rise for ½ hour.
BAKE at 180°C (350°F) for 50-60 minutes.
COOL completely. Sprinkle with icing sugar.

Ferris Wheels

Dough:

350	g	all-purpose flour	2⅓ cups
1	pkg	**oetker** instant dry yeast	1 pkg.
	pinch	salt	pinch
50	g	sugar	¼ cup
1	pkg	**oetker** vanilla sugar	1 pkg.
1		egg	1
1	btl	**oetker** rum flavouring concentrate	1 btl.
80	g	melted butter	⅓ cup
125	mL	lukewarm milk	½ cup

Filling:

50	g	sugar	¼ cup
1	pkg	**oetker** vanilla sugar	1 pkg.
4	g	cinnamon	1 tsp.
50	g	raisins	½ cup
50	g	ground almonds	½ cup
2	sq	semi-sweet chocolate, grated	2 sq.
1		egg white, slightly beaten	1

Glaze:

150	g	sifted icing sugar	1¼ cups
3	drops	**oetker** lemon flavouring concentrate	3 drops
15-30	mL	hot water	1-2 tbsp.

Dough:
PREHEAT oven to 180°C (350°F). Grease a baking sheet.
COMBINE ⅔ of flour, yeast and salt in large mixing bowl. Make a well in centre.
PUT sugar, vanilla sugar, egg, flavouring and melted butter in well.
MIX ingredients, working from centre, gradually adding milk.
BEAT dough until shiny and blistered in appearance.
KNEAD remaining ⅓ of flour into dough until smooth, elastic and no longer sticky.
LET RISE covered in warm place for 30 minutes.
ROLL out dough on floured surface to a rectangle 35 × 45 cm (14″ × 18″).

Filling:
COMBINE sugar, vanilla sugar, cinnamon, raisins, almonds and chocolate.
BRUSH dough with egg white.
SPRINKLE filling evenly over dough.
ROLL up dough starting at longer side.
CUT into slices of 2 cm (¾″) thickness.
PLACE on prepared baking sheet and flatten slightly.
LET RISE in warm place until doubled in size.
BRUSH with egg white.
BAKE on middle oven rack at 180°C (350°F) for 25-30 minutes or until golden. Cool completely.

Glaze:
COMBINE sifted icing sugar, flavouring and enough hot water to make a smooth glaze consistency.
DECORATE ferris wheels with glaze.

Braided Raisin Loaf

Dough:

500 g	all-purpose flour	3⅓ cups
1 pkg	**oetker** instant dry yeast	1 pkg.
pinch	salt	pinch
100 g	sifted icing sugar	¾ cup
1 pkg	**oetker** vanilla sugar	1 pkg.
6	egg yolks	6
1 btl	**oetker** lemon flavouring concentrate	1 btl.
15 mL	rum	1 tbsp.
150 g	melted butter	¾ cup
250 mL	lukewarm milk	1 cup
50 g	raisins	½ cup
1	egg, beaten	1

Decoration:

30 g	coarse sugar	¼ cup

Dough:
PREHEAT oven to 180°C (350°F). Grease a (35 × 15 cm/14″ × 6″) loaf pan.
COMBINE flour, yeast and salt in large bowl. Make a well in centre.
PUT icing sugar, vanilla sugar, egg yolks, flavouring, rum and melted butter in well.
MIX ingredients, working from centre, gradually adding milk.
BEAT dough until shiny and blistered.
LET RISE covered in warm place for 30 minutes.
BEAT down risen dough.
KNEAD raisins into dough.
DIVIDE dough into 3 equal portions and shape each into a roll.
BRAID the three rolls together.
PLACE braided dough into prepared loaf pan.
LET RISE for 30 minutes.
BRUSH loaf with beaten egg.
SPRINKLE with coarse sugar.
BAKE on lower oven rack at 180°C (350°F) for 45-50 minutes or until loaf sounds hollow when lightly tapped.
REMOVE from pan immediately and cool.

Poppyseed Propellers

Dough:

350 g	all-purpose flour	2⅓ cups
1 pkg	**oetker** instant dry yeast	1 pkg.
pinch	salt	pinch
50 g	sugar	¼ cup
1 pkg	**oetker** vanilla sugar	1 pkg.
1	egg	1
2	egg yolks	2
½ btl	**oetker** lemon flavouring	½ btl.
50 g	melted butter	¼ cup
45 mL	lukewarm milk	3 tbsp.

Filling I:

250 g	quark or ricotta cheese	1¼ cups
1	egg yolk	1
50 g	sugar	¼ cup
1 pkg	**oetker** vanilla sugar	1 pkg.
5 drops	**oetker** lemon flavouring	5 drops
30 g	raisins	¼ cup

Filling II:

45 mL	milk	3 tbsp.
50 g	sugar	¼ cup
1 pkg	**oetker** vanilla sugar	1 pkg.
30 mL	liquid honey	2 tbsp.
100 g	ground poppy seeds	1 cup
½ btl	**oetker** rum flavouring	½ btl.
5 drops	**oetker** lemon flavouring	5 drops
pinch	cinnamon	pinch
15 mL	plum jam or marmalade	1 tbsp.

Filling III:

30 mL	plum jam or marmalade	2 tbsp.

Decoration:

6	candied cherries	6

Dough:
PREHEAT oven to 180°C (350°F). Grease a baking sheet.
COMBINE ⅔ of the flour, yeast and salt in large bowl. Make a well in centre.
PUT sugar, vanilla sugar, egg, egg yolks, flavouring and melted butter in well.
MIX ingredients, working from centre, gradually adding milk.
BEAT dough until shiny and blistered.
KNEAD remaining ⅓ flour into dough until smooth, elastic and no longer sticky.
LET RISE covered in a warm place for 15 minutes.
DIVIDE dough into 6 equal portions.
ROLL out each portion to a round (10 cm/4″) in diameter.
PLACE dough on prepared baking sheet. Turn up edges of dough slightly.
Filling I:
COMBINE cheese, egg yolk, sugar, vanilla sugar and flavouring, mixing until smooth.
STIR in raisins.
Filling II:
COMBINE milk, sugar, vanilla sugar and honey in saucepan. Bring to a boil, stirring constantly.
STIR in poppy seeds, flavourings, cinnamon and jam. Cool.
PLACE filling I and filling II alternately on dough round (see picture).
PLACE 1 tsp. of jam in centre of each round.
PLACE a candied cherry on jam.
BAKE on middle oven rack at 180°C (350°F) for 25-30 minutes or until set and golden. Cool.

Poppy Seed Loaf

Dough:

400	g	all-purpose flour	2⅔	cups
1	pkg	**oetker** instant dry yeast	1	pkg.
	pinch	salt		pinch
50	g	ground almonds	½	cup
100	g	sifted icing sugar	¾	cup
1	pkg	**oetker** vanilla sugar	1	pkg.
½	btl	**oetker** lemon flavouring concentrate	½	btl.
1		egg	1	
3		egg yolks	3	
100	g	melted butter	½	cup
180	mL	lukewarm milk	12	tbsp.

Filling:

100	g	sugar	½	cup
1	pkg	**oetker** vanilla sugar	1	pkg.
15	mL	liquid honey	1	tbsp.
15	mL	rum	1	tbsp.
125	mL	milk	½	cup
250	g	ground poppy seeds	2¼	cups
½	btl	**oetker** lemon flavouring concentrate	½	btl.
50	g	raisins	½	cup

Glaze:

200	g	sifted icing sugar	1⅓	cups
5	drops	**oetker** lemon flavouring concentrate	5	drops
30-45	mL	hot water	2-3	tbsp.

Decoration:

ground pistachio nuts

Dough:
PREHEAT oven to 180°C (350°F). Grease a loaf pan.
COMBINE flour, yeast, salt and almonds in large mixing bowl. Make a well in centre.
PUT icing sugar, vanilla sugar, flavouring, egg, egg yolks and melted butter in well.
MIX ingredients, working from centre, gradually adding milk.
BEAT dough until shiny and blistered.
LET RISE covered in warm place until doubled in size, about 30 minutes.
BEAT down risen dough.
ROLL out to 1 cm (½") thickness.
SPREAD filling over dough.
ROLL up starting from both sides simultaneously so that rolls meet in centre.
PLACE dough into prepared loaf pan.
LET RISE again until doubled, about 30 minutes.
BAKE on lower oven rack at 180°C (350°F) for 35-40 minutes or until loaf sounds hollow when lightly tapped.
REMOVE from pan immediately and let cool.
Poppy Seed Filling:
COMBINE sugar, vanilla sugar, honey, rum and milk in saucepan. Bring to a boil, stirring constantly.
STIR in poppy seeds, flavouring and raisins. Cool.
Glaze:
COMBINE sifted icing sugar, flavouring and enough hot water to make a smooth glaze consistency.
SPREAD over top of baked loaf.
SPRINKLE with ground pistachios.

Apricot Filled Doughnuts

Dough:

500	g	all-purpose flour	3⅓	cups
1	pkg	**oetker** instant dry yeast	1	pkg.
	pinch	salt		pinch
50	g	sifted icing sugar	½	cup
1	pkg	**oetker** vanilla sugar	1	pkg.
3		egg yolks	3	
½	btl	**oetker** lemon flavouring concentrate	½	btl.
30	mL	rum	2	tbsp.
100	g	melted butter	½	cup
250	mL	lukewarm milk	1	cup

Dough:
COMBINE flour and yeast in large mixing bowl. Make a well in centre.
PUT salt, icing sugar, vanilla sugar, egg yolks, flavouring, rum and melted butter in well.
WORK flour into centre ingredients, gradually adding milk.
BEAT dough until blistered and shiny in appearance.
LET RISE covered in warm place until doubled in size (about 1 hour).
BEAT down risen dough.
ROLL out on floured surface to 6 mm (¼") thickness.
CUT out with floured round cutter. Make a deep indentation in centre of each round.

Continued on page 82.

For deep frying:
    oil or shortening

Filling:
| 250 mL | apricot jam or marmal- | 1 cup |
| | ade | |

Decoration:
| 1 pkg | **oetker** vanilla sugar | 1 pkg. |
| 25 g | sifted icing sugar | ¼ cup |

HEAT fat to 190°C (375°F).
FRY doughnuts, a few at a time until golden brown on both sides.
REMOVE from fat. Drain on paper towelling.
FILL centres with jam.
COMBINE vanilla sugar and icing sugar.
SPRINKLE over doughnuts.

Recipe No. 157

Cinnamon Fritters

Batter:
250 mL	milk	1 cup
pinch	salt	pinch
1 pkg	**oetker** vanilla sugar	1 pkg.
70 g	butter	⅓ cup
30 mL	rum	2 tbsp.
150 g	all-purpose flour	1 cup
4	eggs	4
2 g	**oetker** baking powder	½ tsp.

For deep frying:
    oil or shortening

Decoration:
100 g	sifted icing sugar	⅔ cup
1 pkg	**oetker** vanilla sugar	1 pkg.
pinch	cinnamon	pinch

Batter:
COMBINE milk, salt, vanilla sugar, butter and rum in saucepan. Bring to a boil.
ADD flour all at once. Cook, stirring vigorously until mixture forms a smooth ball and leaves sides of pan, about 1 minute.
REMOVE from heat. Turn into mixing bowl.
ADD eggs, one at a time, beating well after each addition until smooth and shiny. Cool.
STIR in baking powder.
HEAT fat to 190°C (375°F).
PLACE batter into decorating bag with large star tube.
SQUEEZE desired shapes into fat, a few at a time.
FRY on both sides until golden brown.
REMOVE from fat. Drain on paper towelling.
COMBINE icing sugar, vanilla sugar and cinnamon.
SPRINKLE on fritters. Serve warm.

Chocolate Cream Puffs

Dough:

125 mL	milk	½ cup	
pinch	salt	pinch	
30 g	butter	2 tbsp.	
80 g	all-purpose flour	½ cup	
3	eggs	3	
2 g	**oetker** baking powder	½ tsp.	

Filling:

1 pkg	**oetker** chocolate pudding mix	1 pkg.	
150 g	sugar	¾ cup	
1 btl	**oetker** rum flavouring concentrate	1 btl.	
500 mL	milk	2 cups	
250 g	sweet (unsalted) butter	1 cup	
4 sq	semi-sweet chocolate, melted and cooled	4 sq.	
250 mL	whipping cream	1 cup	
1 pkg	**oetker** Whip it	1 pkg.	

Glaze:

1 pkg	**oetker** Chocofix OR	1 pkg.	
7 sq	semi-sweet chocolate	7 sq.	
100 g	sweet (unsalted) butter	½ cup	

Dough:
PREHEAT oven to 200°C (400°F). Grease and flour a baking sheet.
COMBINE milk, salt and butter in saucepan. Bring to a boil.
ADD flour all at once. Cook, stirring vigorously until mixture forms a smooth ball and leaves sides of pan, about 1 minute.
REMOVE from heat. Turn into mixing bowl.
ADD eggs, one at a time, beating well after each addition until smooth and shiny. Cool.
STIR in baking powder.
PUT dough into decorating bag with large round tube.
SQUEEZE small rounds onto prepared baking sheet.
BAKE on middle oven rack at 200°C (400°F) for 30-35 minutes or until golden.
DO NOT OPEN oven during first 15 minutes of baking.
CUT puffs in half horizontally immediately after baking.
Filling:
COMBINE pudding mix, sugar, rum flavouring concentrate and 125 mL (½ cup) milk in small bowl. Stir until smoothly blended.
RINSE saucepan with cold water.
HEAT remaining 375 mL (1½ cups) milk to boiling. Stir in pudding mixture. Bring to boil again, stirring constantly.
REMOVE from heat. Cool to room temperature, stirring occasionally.
CREAM butter. Beat in pudding and chocolate 1 spoonful at a time. (Butter, chocolate and pudding must be at same temperature to prevent curdling.)
BEAT whipping cream to soft peaks. Gradually add Whip it, beating to stiff peaks.
FOLD whipped cream into pudding mixture.
FILL bottom of puffs with cream mixture.
PLACE tops over filling.
Glaze:
PREPARE Chocofix according to directions on package OR combine chocolate and butter in top of double boiler PLACE over boiling water, stirring constantly until smoothly melted.
SPREAD glaze over cream puff tops.

Cheese Filled Vol-au-vents

Dough:

250 mL	water	1 cup	
pinch	salt	pinch	
50 g	butter or margarine	¼ cup	
100 g	all-purpose flour	⅔ cup	
4	eggs	4	
4 g	**oetker** baking powder	1 tsp.	

Filling:

1 pkg	**oetker** cheesecake filling mix	1 pkg.	
500 mL	water	2 cups	
500 g	strained quark, ricotta or creamed cottage cheese	2 cups	
250 mL	whipping cream	1 cup	

Dough:
PREHEAT oven to 200°C (400°F). Grease and flour a baking sheet.
COMBINE water, salt and butter in a saucepan. Bring to a boil.
ADD flour all at once. Cook, stirring vigorously until mixture leaves sides of pan, about 1 minute.
REMOVE from heat. Turn into mixing bowl.
ADD eggs, one at a time, beating well after each addition until smooth and shiny. Cool.
STIR in baking powder.

Continued on page 86.

84

Cheese Filled Vol-au-vents (cont.)

Filling:

1 pkg	**oetker** cheesecake filling mix	1 pkg.
500 mL	water	2 cups
500 g	strained quark, ricotta or creamed cottage cheese	2 cups
250 mL	whipping cream	1 cup

Dough:
DROP batter by spoonfuls in 5 cm (2″) rounds onto prepared baking sheet. OR squeeze through a decorating bag with large round tube.
BAKE on middle oven rack at 200°C (400°F) for 30-35 minutes or until golden. Do not open oven doo during first 15 minutes baking.
CUT in half horizontally immediately after baking.
Filling:
COMBINE cheesecake filling mix and water and bea until foamy.
MIX cheese until smooth. Gradually add to prepared filling mixture.
BEAT whipping cream to stiff peaks. Fold into chees mixture.
FILL bottom of puffs with cream cheese mixture.
PLACE tops over filling.

Recipe No. 160

Giant Pizza

Dough:

350 g	all-purpose flour	2⅓ cups
1 pkg	**oetker** instant dry yeast	1 pkg.
pinch	salt	pinch
150 mL	lukewarm water	10 tbsp.
180 mL	olive oil	12 tbsp.

Seafood and Olive Filling:

45 mL	tomatoe paste	3 tbsp.
100 g	mussels	4 oz.
100 g	anchovy fillets	4 oz.
2-3	tomatoes, thinly sliced	2-3
100 g	mozzarella cheese	4 oz.
12	green or black olives	12
	grated parmesan cheese	
	oregano	
	capers	

Bacon and Mushroom Filling:

45 mL	tomato paste	3 tbsp.
100 g	bacon, diced	¼ lb.
150 g	mushrooms	5½ oz.
3	tomatoes, thinly sliced	3
100 g	mozzarella cheese	4 oz.
	oregano, parsley	
	grated parmesan cheese	

Vegetable Filling:

45 mL	tomato paste	3 tbsp.
1 can	artichokes	1 can
100 g	bacon, diced	4 oz.
2-3	tomatoes, thinly sliced	2-3
30-50 g	salami	2 oz.
1	green pepper	1
100 g	mozzarella cheese	4 oz.
1	small onion	1
6	stuffed olives, sliced	6
	oregano	
	grated parmesan cheese	

Dough:
PREHEAT oven to 200°C (400°F). Grease baking sheets or pizza pans.
COMBINE ⅔ of flour and yeast in large bowl.
ADD salt, water and olive oil. Stir until all ingredien are well blended.
KNEAD until shiny and blistered in appearance.
KNEAD remaining flour into mixture.
LET RISE covered in warm place.
DIVIDE dough into 3 equal portions.
ROLL out each portion to a 25-30 cm (10″-12″) circl
PLACE on prepared baking sheets.
BRUSH lightly with olive oil and spread with tomato paste.
Filling:
CUT ingredients into small pieces or thin slices.
DISTRIBUTE evenly over dough in listed sequence.
SPRINKLE with seasonings and parmesan cheese.
BAKE on middle oven rack at 200°C (400°F) for 20-25 minutes or until crust is golden and filling is he

Cheese Casserole

Pastry:

40 g	butter	¼	cup
4	egg yolks	4	
50 g	all-purpose flour	⅓	cup
8 g	**oetker** baking powder	2	tsp.
75 mL	sour cream	⅓	cup
150 g	diced ham	5	oz.
125 g	grated Swiss cheese	4	oz.
4	egg whites	4	

Glaze:

30 g	grated parmesan cheese	1	oz.
	butter		

Pastry:
PREHEAT oven to 180°C (350°F). Grease several
small casserole dishes or one large one.
CREAM butter. Gradually add egg yolks, flour and
baking powder.
ADD sour cream, one tablespoon at a time. Mix well.
FOLD in ham and cheese.
BEAT egg whites to stiff peaks.
FOLD into cheese mixture.
TURN mixture into greased casseroles.
SPRINKLE with grated parmesan cheese.
DOT with small pieces of butter.
BAKE on middle oven rack at 180°C (350°F) for
30-35 minutes or until set.
SERVE hot.

Ham Rounds

Dough:

300 g	all-purpose flour	2	cups
1 pkg	**oetker** instant dry yeast	1	pkg.
4 g	salt	1	tsp.
2	egg yolks	2	
140 g	melted butter	⅔	cup
30 mL	sour cream	2	tbsp.
45-60 mL	lukewarm milk	3-4	tbsp.

Filling:

150 g	diced ham	5	oz.
30 g	grated smoked cheese	1	oz.
pinch	salt		pinch
pinch	paprika		pinch
15-30 mL	sour cream	1-2	tbsp.
1	egg yolk, beaten	1	

Dough:
PREHEAT oven to 180°C (350°F). Grease a baking
sheet.
COMBINE ⅔ of flour and yeast in large bowl. Make a
well in centre.
PUT salt, egg yolks, butter and sour cream in well.
Working form centre, stir until all ingredients are well
blended.
ADD milk gradually.
KNEAD until shiny and blistered in appearance.
KNEAD remaining ⅓ of flour into mixture.
LET RISE covered in warm place until doubled in size
(about 30 minutes).
Filling:
COMBINE all ingredients in bowl. Mix well.
BEAT down risen dough.
ROLL out on floured surface to 6 mm (¼") thickness.
CUT out rounds 8 cm (3") in diameter with floured
cutter.
PLACE filling on half of the rounds, dividing evenly.
COVER with remaining rounds.
PRESS to seal seams. Place on prepared baking sheet.
LET rise in warm place until doubled (about
30 minutes).
BRUSH with egg yolk.
BAKE at 180°C (350°F) for 35-40 minutes or until
golden.
SERVE hot.

Spiced Cheese Filled Vol-au-vents

Pastry:

125	mL	water	½ cup
20	g	butter	2 tbsp.
	pinch	salt	pinch
	pinch	nutmeg	pinch
100	g	all-purpose flour	⅔ cup
3		eggs	3
	pinch	**oetker** baking powder	pinch

Cream Cheese Filling:

150	g	butter or margarine	¾ cup
250	g	cream cheese	8 oz.
1		egg yolk	1
30	mL	cognac	2 tbsp.
	pinch	cayenne pepper	pinch
15	mL	finely chopped chives, parsley and olives	1 tbsp.

Decoration:

	stuffed green olives

Pastry:
PREHEAT oven to 200°C (400°F). Grease and flour a baking sheet.
COMBINE water, butter, salt, and nutmeg in saucepan. Bring to a boil.
ADD flour all at once. Cook, stirring vigorously until mixture forms a smooth ball and leaves sides of pan, about 1 minute.
REMOVE from heat. Turn into mixing bowl.
ADD eggs, one at a time, beating well after each addition until smooth and shiny. Cool.
STIR in baking powder.
PLACE pastry in decorating bag with large round tube.
SQUEEZE small rounds onto prepared baking sheet.
BAKE on middle oven rack at 200°C (400°F) for 30-35 minutes or until golden.
DO NOT OPEN oven during first 15 minutes of baking time.
CUT top off each round immediately after baking.
Filling:
COMBINE butter, cream cheese, egg yolk, cognac and cayenne pepper.
STIR until well blended.
FOLD chives, parsley and chopped olives into mixture. Mix well.
SPREAD most of filling on bottom of puffs. Place tops over filling.
DECORATE with remaining filling and olives.

Cheese Munchies

Dough:

150	g	all-purpose flour	1 cup
	pinch	**oetker** baking powder	pinch
150	g	cream cheese	¾ cup
1		egg	1
2	g	salt	½ tsp.
150	g	butter, cold	¾ cup

Decoration:

30	g	grated parmesan cheese	¼ cup
		salt	
		caraway seeds	
		paprika	

Dough:
PREHEAT oven to 200°C (400°F). Grease a baking sheet.
SIFT flour and baking powder onto pastry board. Make a well in centre.
PUT cheese, egg and salt in well. Work a little flour into mixture.
CUT cold butter into small pieces over flour mixture.
WORK all ingredients together quickly into a smooth dough. Chill ½ hour for easy rolling.
ROLL out dough into a rectangle 6 mm (¼") thick.
FOLD sides of dough into centre.
CHILL 10 minutes.
REPEAT rolling, folding and chilling 2 more times.
ROLL out dough to 6 mm (¼") thickness.
CUT out desired shapes with floured cutter.
SPRINKLE with grated parmesan cheese, salt, caraway seeds and paprika.
PLACE onto prepared baking sheet.
BAKE on middle oven rack at 200°C (400°F) for 10-15 minutes or until golden.

Potato Bread

Dough:

500 g	all-purpose flour	3⅓ cups	
1 pkg	**oetker** instant dry yeast	1 pkg.	
pinch	salt	pinch	
250 g	cooked mashed potatoes, cold	1¼ cups	
80 g	sugar	⅓ cup	
3	egg yolks	3	
50 g	melted butter	¼ cup	
125 mL	lukewarm milk	½ cup	
120 g	raisins	1 cup	

Dough:
PREHEAT oven to 180°C (350°F). Grease a baking sheet.
COMBINE flour, yeast and salt in large bowl or on pastry board.
PLACE potatoes over flour mixture. Make a well in centre.
PUT sugar, egg yolks and melted butter in well.
Working from centre, stir until all ingredients are well blended, adding milk gradually.
LET RISE covered in a warm place for 30 minutes.
ADD raisins.
KNEAD again thoroughly.
SHAPE dough into a loaf.
PLACE on prepared baking sheet.
LET RISE again until doubled in size.
BAKE on middle oven rack at 180°C (350°F) for 40-45 minutes or until golden.

Aniseed Loaf

Batter:

2	egg yolks	2	
100 g	sugar	½ cup	
1 pkg	**oetker** vanilla sugar	1 pkg.	
½ btl	**oetker** lemon flavouring concentrate	½ btl.	
300 g	cooked, mashed potatoes	1½ cups	
45 mL	milk	3 tbsp.	
2	egg whites	2	
200 g	all-purpose flour	1⅓ cups	
1 pkg	**oetker** baking powder (14 g/1 tbsp.)	1 pkg.	
pinch	salt	pinch	
30 g	raisins	¼ cup	
10 g	aniseed	⅓ oz.	

Batter:
PREHEAT oven to 180°C (350°F). Grease a loaf pan.
COMBINE egg yolks, ⅔ of sugar, vanilla sugar and flavouring in mixer bowl.
BEAT at high speed of electric mixer until thick and creamy.
STIR in mashed potatoes and milk.
BEAT egg whites and remaining sugar to stiff peaks.
FOLD into egg yolk mixture.
SIFT flour and baking powder over egg mixture.
ADD raisins and aniseed.
FOLD all ingredients together and until well blended.
TURN batter into prepared pan.
BAKE on lower oven rack at 180°C (350°F) for 50-60 minutes or until golden.

Red Currant Triangles

Dough:

250 g	all-purpose flour	1⅔ cups	
1 pkg	**oetker** baking powder (14 g/1 tbsp.)	1 pkg.	
pinch	salt	pinch	
200 g	cooked, mashed potatoes	1 cup	
1	egg	1	
120 g	sugar	½ cup	
1 pkg	**oetker** vanilla sugar	1 pkg.	
½ btl	**oetker** lemon flavouring concentrate	½ btl.	
120 g	butter, cold	½ cup	

Filling:

125 mL	red currant jam or jelly	½ cup	
50 g	ground hazelnuts	½ cup	

Dough:
PREHEAT oven to 180°C (350°F). Grease a 2 L (39 cm × 26 cm/15" × 10") jelly roll pan.
SIFT flour and baking powder together on pastry board.
ADD salt and cold mashed potatoes. Make a well in centre.
PUT egg, sugar, vanilla sugar and flavouring in well. Mix small amount of flour mixture into centre ingredients to make a thick paste.
CUT cold butter into small pieces over flour mixture. Working quickly from the centre, work all ingredients together to make a smooth dough. Chill 30 minutes for easy rolling.
PRESS or ROLL ½ of dough into prepared pan.
SPREAD with half of jam.
SPRINKLE with ground hazelnuts.
ROLL out remaining dough. Place over filling.
BAKE on middle oven rack at 180°C (350°F) for 35-45 minutes or until golden.
SPREAD remaining jam over hot cake.
LET cool completely.
CUT into triangles.

Hazelnut Slices

Dough:

2	eggs	2	
200 g	sugar	1 cup	
1 pkg	**oetker** vanilla sugar	1 pkg.	
½ btl	**oetker** lemon flavouring concentrate	½ btl.	
100 g	cooked, mashed potatoes	½ cup	
100 g	ground hazelnuts	1 cup	
80 g	all-purpose flour	⅔ cup	
1 pkg	**oetker** baking powder (14 g/1 tbsp.)	1 pkg.	

Glaze:

250 g	sifted icing sugar	2 cups	
	juice of ½ lemon		
15-30 mL	hot water	1-2 tbsp.	
15 mL	rum	1 tbsp.	

Dough:
PREHEAT oven to 180°C (350°F). Grease a 2 L (39 cm × 26 cm/15" × 10") jelly roll pan.
COMBINE eggs, sugar, vanilla sugar and flavouring in mixer bowl. Beat at high speed of electric mixer until thick and creamy.
ADD mashed potatoes and ground hazelnuts to egg mixture.
SIFT flour and baking powder over mixture.
FOLD all ingredients together until well blended.
PRESS dough onto prepared pan.
BAKE on middle oven rack at 180°C (350°F) for 35-40 minutes or until golden.
LET cool completely.
Glaze:
BLEND icing sugar, lemon juice, hot water and rum to make a smooth glaze consistency.
SPREAD over cake. Let icing set.
CUT into slices to serve.

Almond Potato Fritters

Dough:

250 g	cooked, mashed potatoes	1¼	cups
4 g	salt	1	tsp.
3	egg yolks	3	
100 g	ground almonds	1	cup
125 mL	milk	½	cup
250 g	all-purpose flour	1⅔	cups
1 pkg	**oetker** baking powder (14g/1tbsp.)	1	pkg.
3	egg whites	3	
30 g	sugar	3	tbsp.
	icing sugar		

For deep frying:

oil or shortening

Dough:

COMBINE potatoes, salt, egg yolks, ground almonds and milk in large bowl. Blend well.

SIFT flour and baking powder over potato mixture.

WORK dough until smooth, shiny and blistered in appearance. If required, add a little more milk.

BEAT egg whites to soft peaks. Gradually add sugar, beating to stiff peaks.

FOLD into dough gently.

HEAT fat to 190°C (375°F).

DROP dough by small spoonfuls into hot fat.

FRY, a few at a time, until golden brown on both sides.

REMOVE from fat. Drain on paper towelling.

SPRINKLE with icing sugar.

SERVE warm.

Potato Croquettes

Dough:

500 g	potatoes	1	lb.
1	egg, beaten	1	
30 g	grated parmesan cheese	¼	cup
pinch	salt	pinch	
pinch	ground nutmeg	pinch	
2 g	**oetker** baking powder	½	tsp.

Breading:

80 g	all-purpose flour	½	cup
1	egg, beaten	1	
150 g	fine dry bread crumbs	1½	cups

For deep frying:

oil or shortening

Dough:

PEEL potatoes.

COOK in salted water just until tender. Do not overcook.

DRAIN and mash.

COMBINE warm potatoes, egg, parmesan cheese, salt, nutmeg and baking powder.

KNEAD into a smooth dough.

SHAPE dough into logs 5 cm (2") long.

ROLL logs in flour. Dip in egg and roll in bread crumbs.

HEAT fat to 190°C (375°F).

FRY croquettes until golden brown on all sides.

DRAIN on paper towelling.

SERVE hot.

Jamaica Fruit Flip

1	pkg	**oetker** vanilla mousse	1 pkg.
250	mL	cold milk	1 cup
15	mL	rum	1 tbsp.
15	mL	apricot brandy	1 tbsp.
125	mL	whipping cream	½ cup
½	pkg	**oetker** Whip it	½ pkg.
½	pkg	**oetker** vanilla sugar	½ pkg.
500	mL	strawberry ice cream	½ cup

Decoration:

fruit as desired

COMBINE mousse with milk.
PREPARE according to package directions.
STIR in rum and apricot brandy.
SPOON into dessert dishes.
BEAT whipping cream to soft peaks. Gradually add
Whip it and vanilla sugar, beating to stiff peaks.
PLACE 3 small scoops of ice cream on mousse.
DECORATE dessert attractively with whipped cream
and fruit.
CHILL until serving.

Diplomat Cream

50	g	raisins	½ cup
15	mL	rum	1 tbsp.
1	pkg	**oetker** vanilla mousse	1 pkg.
250	mL	cold milk	1 cup
10		lady fingers	10
75	mL	cherry brandy	⅓ cup
2	sq	semi-sweet chocolate, grated	2 sq.

Decoration:

whipped cream
maraschino cherries

COMBINE raisins and rum. Bring to a boil. Let cool
COMBINE mousse with milk.
PREPARE according to package directions.
SPOON half of mousse into dessert dishes.
PLACE lady fingers on mousse.
SPRINKLE with cherry brandy.
SPRINKLE soaked raisins and grated chocolate over
lady fingers.
SPOON remaining vanilla mousse on top.
DECORATE top with whipped cream and cherries.
CHILL until serving.

Hawaiian Cocktail

1	pkg	**oetker** strawberry or raspberry mousse	1 pkg.
200	mL	cold milk	¾ cup
30	mL	cherry liqueur	2 tbsp.
30	mL	apricot brandy	2 tbsp.
1		whole pineapple	1
200	g	fresh or canned fruit (strawberries, raspberries, kiwis, mandarins, etc.)	7 oz.
1	pkg	**oetker** vanilla sugar	1 pkg.

Decoration:

125	mL	whipping cream	½ cup
½	pkg	**oetker** Whip it	½ pkg.
½	pkg	**oetker** vanilla sugar	½ pkg.

COMBINE mousse with milk.
PREPARE according to package directions.
STIR in cherry liqueur and apricot brandy.
CUT pineapple into halves.
SCOOP out carefully leaving a shell.
DICE fruit.
COMBINE pineapple, other fruit and vanilla sugar.
FILL pineapple halves with mousse.
PLACE fruit on top.
BEAT whipping cream to soft peaks. Gradually add
Whip it and vanilla sugar, beating to stiff peaks.
DECORATE pineapple halves attractively with
whipped cream.
CHILL until serving.

Black Forest Parfait

Ingredients:

1 pkg	**oetker** vanilla mousse	1 pkg.	
250 mL	cold milk	1 cup	
1 can	sweet cherries (398 mL / 14 oz), pitted	1 can	
50 mL	cherry brandy	¼ cup	

Decoration:

125 mL	whipping cream	½ cup	
½ pkg	**oetker** Whip it	½ pkg.	
½ pkg	**oetker** vanilla sugar	½ pkg.	
2 sq	semi-sweet chocolate, grated	2 sq.	

Method:
COMBINE vanilla mousse with milk.
PREPARE according to package directions. Chill.
DRAIN cherries and mix with cherry brandy.
SPOON 30 mL (2 tbsp.) cherries into parfait glasses.
COVER with mousse.
Decoration:
BEAT whipping cream to soft peaks. Gradually add Whip it and vanilla sugar, beating to stiff peaks.
DECORATE dessert attractively with whipped cream and grated chocolate.
CHILL until serving.

Apricot Delight

Ingredients:

1 pkg	**oetker** vanilla mousse	1 pkg.	
250 mL	cold milk	1 cup	
30 mL	apricot brandy	2 tbsp.	

Decoration:

canned apricot halves
whipped cream, optional

Method:
COMBINE vanilla mousse with milk.
PREPARE according to package directions.
STIR in apricot brandy.
SPOON into dessert dishes.
DECORATE with apricot halves and whipped cream.
CHILL until serving.

Chocolate Marzipan Dessert

Ingredients:

3	canned apricots or peaches	3	
100 g	almond paste	3½ oz.	
1 pkg	**oetker** chocolate mousse	1 pkg.	
250 mL	cold milk	1 cup	
6 drops	**oetker** rum flavouring concentrate	6 drops	

Decoration:

125 mL	whipping cream	½ cup	
½ pkg	**oetker** Whip it	½ pkg.	
½ pkg	**oetker** vanilla sugar	½ pkg.	
	semi-sweet chocolate, grated		

Method:
CUT fruit and almond paste into small pieces.
COMBINE chocolate mousse with milk.
PREPARE according to package directions.
STIR in rum flavouring.
FOLD fruit and almond paste into mousse.
SPOON into dessert dishes.
Decoration:
BEAT whipping cream to soft peaks. Gradually add Whip it and vanilla sugar, beating to stiff peaks.
DECORATE dessert attractively with whipped cream and grated chocolate.
CHILL until serving.

Recipe No. 177

Strawberries "Romanoff"

Ingredients:

1	pkg	**oetker** chocolate mousse	1	pkg.
250	mL	cold milk	1	cup
250	g	fresh or frozen strawberries	8	oz.
50	mL	cherry brandy	¼	cup

Decoration:

125	mL	whipping cream	½	cup
½	pkg	**oetker** Whip it	½	pkg.
½	pkg	**oetker** vanilla sugar	½	pkg.

Method:
COMBINE mousse with milk.
PREPARE according to package directions.
SPOON strawberries into tall glasses.
SPRINKLE with cherry brandy.
SPOON chocolate mousse over fruit.
Decoration:
BEAT whipping cream to soft peaks. Gradually add Whip it and vanilla sugar, beating to stiff peaks.
DECORATE desserts with whipped cream and strawberries.

Recipe No. 178

Chocolate Raspberry Delight

Ingredients:

1	pkg	**oetker** chocolate mousse	1	pkg.
250	mL	cold milk	1	cup
10-12		meringue shells	10-12	
45	mL	cherry brandy	3	tbsp.

Decoration:

1	pint	raspberries	2	cups
1	pkg	**oetker** vanilla sugar	1	pkg.
30	mL	cherry brandy	2	tbsp.
125	mL	whipping cream	½	cup
½	pkg	**oetker** Whip it	½	pkg.
½	pkg	**oetker** vanilla sugar	½	pkg.

Method:
COMBINE chocolate mousse with milk.
PREPARE according to package directions.
BREAK some of the meringue shells into small pieces.
PLACE into dessert dishes.
SPRINKLE with cherry brandy.
SPOON chocolate mousse over meringue.
PLACE a whole meringue shell on mousse in each dish.
Decoration:
COMBINE raspberries, vanilla sugar and cherry brandy.
Reserve some raspberries for decoration.
FILL into meringue shells.
BEAT whipping cream to soft peaks. Gradually add Whip it and vanilla sugar, beating to stiff peaks.
DECORATE dessert attractively with whipped cream.
Chill until serving.

Recipe No. 179

Apple Blankets with Blueberry Cream

Apple Blankets:

100	g	all-purpose flour	⅔	cup
	pinch	**oetker** baking powder		pinch
4		egg yolks	4	
2	pkg	**oetker** vanilla sugar	2	pkg.
	pinch	salt		pinch
125	mL	cold mineral water	½	cup
500	g	apples	1	lb.
		juice of ½ lemon		
4		egg whites	4	

For frying:

		butter

Blueberry Cream:

1	pkg	**oetker** vanilla mousse	1	pkg.
125	mL	milk	½	cup
125	mL	blueberry juice	½	cup
30	mL	rum	2	tbsp.

Decoration:

		icing sugar

Method:
Apple Blankets:
COMBINE flour and baking powder in mixing bowl.
Make a well in centre.
PUT egg yolks, vanilla sugar and salt into well. Work into a smooth dough, gradually adding mineral water, 15 mL (1 tbsp.) at a time.
PEEL and core apples. Grate coarsely.
SPRINKLE with lemon juice.
BEAT egg whites to stiff peaks.
FOLD egg whites and apples into batter.
HEAT butter in an omelette pan or frying pan.
POUR 50 mL (¼ cup) batter into pan and cook on both sides till golden brown.
Blueberry Cream:
COMBINE mousse with milk and blueberry juice.
PREPARE according to package directions.
STIR in rum.
SPRINKLE warm apple blankets with icing sugar.
SERVE with blueberry cream.

Mocha Cherry Dessert

1 pkg	**oetker** mocha mousse	1 pkg.	
250 mL	cold milk	1 cup	
125 mL	whipping cream	½ cup	
½ pkg	**oetker** Whip it	½ pkg.	
½ pkg	**oetker** vanilla sugar	½ pkg.	
125 mL	drained canned cherries	½ cup	
	cherry brandy, optional		

COMBINE mousse with milk.
PREPARE according to package directions.
SPOON mocha mousse into dessert dishes. Chill.
BEAT whipping cream to soft peaks. Gradually add
Whip it and vanilla sugar, beating to stiff peaks.
SPRINKLE cherries with cherry brandy if desired.
DECORATE dessert attractively with whipping cream
and cherries.
CHILL until serving.

Chocolate Cream Dessert

1 pkg	**oetker** chocolate pudding mix	1 pkg.	
500 mL	milk	2 cups	

Topping:

125 mL	whipping cream	½ cup	
½ pkg	**oetker** Whip it	½ pkg.	
1 pkg	**oetker** vanilla sugar	1 pkg.	
	egg liqueur, optional		
	maraschino cherries		

COMBINE chocolate pudding mix with milk.
PREPARE according to package directions.
SPOON into dessert glasses. Chill.
BEAT whipping cream to soft peaks. Gradually add
Whip it and vanilla sugar, beating to stiff peaks.
SPRINKLE egg liqueur over pudding, if desired.
DECORATE pudding with whipped cream and
cherries.
CHILL until serving.

Surprise Omelette

Batter:

3	egg yolks	3
80 g	sugar	⅓ cup
1 pkg	**oetker** vanilla sugar	1 pkg.
3	egg whites	3
40 g	all-purpose flour	¼ cup
pinch	**oetker** baking powder	pinch
	butter for frying	

Filling:

apricot jam
canned fruit, as desired
rum or brandy

COMBINE egg yolks, sugar and vanilla sugar in small mixer bowl.
BEAT at high speed of electric mixer until thick and creamy.
BEAT egg whites to stiff peaks.
SIFT flour and baking powder together over egg yolk mixture and fold in gently.
FOLD in egg whites gently.
HEAT butter in omelette pan.
SPOON about 125 mL (½ cup) batter into omelette pan. Spread lightly to a circle.
BAKE until golden brown on both sides. Keep warm.
REPEAT with remaining batter.
SPREAD jam over omelette.
COVER with fruit.
SPRINKLE rum over fruit.
FLAME if desired.

Witches' Mousse

1 pkg	**oetker** chocolate mousse	1 pkg.
250 mL	cold milk	1¼ cups
1	egg white	1
1 pkg	**oetker** vanilla sugar	1 pkg.
50 g	sifted icing sugar	½ cup
125 g	raspberries or strawberries	4 oz.

Method:
COMBINE mousse with milk.
PREPARE according to package directions.
SPOON into dessert glasses, to about ¾ full.
BEAT egg white to soft peaks. Gradually add vanilla sugar and icing sugar, beating to stiff peaks.
FOLD berries into egg white mixture. Blend well.
SPOON over chocolate mousse.
CHILL until serving.

Brandied Fruit Delight

Ingredients:

1 pkg	**oetker** vanilla pudding mix	1 pkg.
500 mL	milk	2 cups
50 g	sugar	¼ cup
30 mL	brandy or cognac	2 tbsp.
150 g	chopped candied fruit and nuts	½ cup

Decoration:

125 mL	whipping cream	½ cup
½ pkg	**oetker** Whip it	½ pkg.
½ pkg	**oetker** vanilla sugar	½ pkg.

Method:
COMBINE vanilla pudding mix with milk.
PREPARE according to package directions.
SPOON into dessert dishes.
SPRINKLE with chopped candied fruit and nuts.
BEAT whipping cream to soft peaks. Gradually add Whip it and vanilla sugar, beating to stiff peaks.
DECORATE puddings attractively with whipped cream.
CHILL until serving.

Viennese Mocha Dessert

1	pkg	**oetker** mocha mousse	1	pkg.
250	mL	cold milk	1	cup

Decoration:

125	mL	whipping cream	½	cup
½	pkg	**oetker** Whip it	½	pkg.
1	pkg	**oetker** vanilla sugar	1	pkg.
4-6		meringue shells	4-6	
		mocha liqueur		

Method:
COMBINE mocha mousse with milk.
PREPARE according to package directions.
SPOON into dessert dishes.
BEAT whipping cream to soft peaks. Gradually add Whip it and vanilla sugar, beating to stiff peaks.
PLACE one meringue shell on mousse in each dish. Fill with whipped cream.
SPRINKLE with mocha liqueur.
CHILL until serving.

Mocha Parfait

Method:

1	pkg	**oetker** vanilla mousse	1	pkg.
1	pkg	**oetker** mocha mousse	1	pkg.
500	mL	cold milk	2	cups
		mocha liqueur to taste		
		whipped cream		
		chocolate covered coffee beans		

Method:
PREPARE vanilla mousse and mocha mousse separately according to package directions.
SPOON vanilla mousse and mocha mousse in alternate layers into parfait dishes ending with the vanilla.
CHILL.
JUST before serving, pour mocha liqueur over each serving.
DECORATE with whipped cream and coffee beans.

Florentine Nut Dessert

1	pkg	**oetker** butterscotch mousse	1	pkg.
250	mL	cold milk	1	cup
30	g	ground peanuts or almonds	⅓	cup

Decoration:

125	mL	whipping cream	½	cup
1	pkg	**oetker** Whip it	1	pkg.
1	pkg	**oetker** vanilla sugar	1	pkg.
		mandarin oranges		
4-6		small florentine cookies	4-6	

Method:
COMBINE butterscotch mousse and milk.
PREPARE according to package directions.
SPOON into dessert dishes.
SPRINKLE with ground nuts.
BEAT whipping cream to soft peaks. Gradually add Whip it and vanilla sugar, beating to stiff peaks.
DECORATE attractively with whipped cream, mandarins and cookies.

Pink Party Dessert

1	pkg	**oetker** raspberry OR strawberry mousse	1 pkg.
250	mL	cold milk	1 cup
		fruit juice OR liqueur to taste	
		coarse sugar	
		orange slices	

Method:
COMBINE raspberry mousse with milk.
PREPARE according to package directions.
DIP parfait glasses first in fruit juice or liqueur, then in sugar. Let dry.
SPOON mousse into glasses carefully.
DECORATE each glass with an orange slice.

Almond Crunch

Ingredients:

1	pkg	**oetker** vanilla pudding mix	1 pkg.
50	g	sugar	¼ cup
500	mL	white wine	2 cups
250	mL	whipping cream	1 cup

Decoration:

30	g	chopped almonds	¼ cup
30	g	sugar	2 tbsp.
10	g	sweet (unsalted) butter	1 tsp.
		whipped cream, optional	
		maraschino cherries, optional	

Method:
COMBINE vanilla pudding mix, sugar and 125 mL (½ cup) wine in small bowl. Stir until smoothly blended.
HEAT remaining wine to boiling. Stir in pudding mixture. Bring to boil again, stirring constantly.
REMOVE from heat. Cool to room temperature, stirring occasionally.
BEAT whipping cream to stiff peaks.
FOLD into pudding mixture.
SPOON into dessert dishes.
Decoration:
COMBINE almonds, sugar and butter in saucepan.
HEAT until golden brown, stirring constantly. Let cool.
CHOP finely.
SPRINKLE almond mixture over pudding.
DECORATE with whipped cream and maraschino cherries, if desired.

Banana Split

1	pkg	**oetker** chocolate mousse	1 pkg.
250	mL	cold milk	1 cup
4		bananas	4
30	mL	lemon juice	2 tbsp.
3	pkg	**oetker** vanilla sugar	3 pkg.

Decoration:

125	mL	whipping cream	½ cup
½	pkg	**oetker** Whip it	½ pkg.
½	pkg	**oetker** vanilla sugar	½ pkg.
50	g	sliced toasted almonds	½ cup
		vanilla ice cream	
		mandarin oranges	
		shaved chocolate	

Method:
COMBINE mousse with milk.
PREPARE according to package directions.
PEEL and half bananas lengthwise.
MARINATE bananas in mixture of lemon juice and vanilla sugar.
PLACE two banana halves into one long dessert dish.
SPOON mousse between the banana halves.
BEAT whipping cream to soft peaks. Gradually add Whip it and vanilla sugar, beating to stiff peaks.
DECORATE banana split with whipped cream, toasted almonds, small scoops of ice cream, mandarin and shaved chocolate.

TOP QUALITY — made from the best and, wherever possible, natural ingredients

CONVENIENCE — premeasured packages make baking easier and worry free

FRESHNESS — tightly sealed and coated individual packages guarantee freshness every time you use them.

oetker Baking Powder
Baked goods obtain a light and tender, fine, even texture. **oetker** Baking Powder leaves no after taste. Individual, premeasured, coated and tightly sealed pouches guarantee freshness and success every time.

oetker Vanilla Sugar
It blends instantly and uniformly in dry as well as liquid ingredients. There is no colour change with the **oetker** product as there is with the brown liquid vanilla. No measuring required — just sprinkle.

oetker Natural Vanilla Sugar
Is produced from the extract of vanilla beans. It has the true rich, smooth, full taste that your baking deserves.

oetker Instant Dry Yeast
Requires no refrigeration. It is mixed directly with the flour, eliminating the pre-mixing with liquid step. Its increased rising power will also save time.

oetker Whip it
Keeps whipped cream stiff and appetizing for hours. **Whip it** is completely neutral in colour and taste.

oetker Glaze (clear and red)
Is easy to prepare and sets fast. Its sparkling clear appearance enhances and preserves the colour, flavour and freshness of fruit flans.

oetker Pudding and Pie Fillings
Are quick and easy to prepare. They are smooth and creamy in a variety of delicious flavours: Chocolate, Vanilla, Strawberry, Raspberry, Cream, Lemon and Almond.

oetker Mousse
Is a creamy, light, tasty dessert that sets instantly. It's easy to prepare in one easy mixing step with no cooking required. **oetker** Mousse comes in a variety of favourite flavours.

oetker Chocofix
Is a beautiful chocolate frosting and glaze that is extremely quick, easy and convenient to prepare. The foil pouch is softened in boiling water then poured directly onto your cake dessert. Dutch cocoa powder gives **Chocofix** its unique full, rich European chocolate flavour.

oetker Flavouring Concentrates
Retain the true, natural flavour and aroma during baking. They are easy and convenient to use and are four times more concentrated than regular flavourings.

Notes

Notes